RESEARCH BIBLIOGRAPHIES & CHECKLISTS

8

Eugène Fromentin

RESEARCH BIBLIOGRAPHIES & CHECKLISTS

RCB

Edited by

A. D. Deyermond, J. R. Little and J. E. Varey

EUGÈNE FROMENTIN

a bibliography

BARBARA WRIGHT

Grant & Cutler Ltd

1973

ISBN 0 900411 73 2

I.S.B.N. 84-399-1670-1

DEPÓSITO LEGAL: V. 3.988 - 1973

Printed in Spain by
Artes Gráficas Soler, S.A., Valencia

for

GRANT & CUTLER LTD
11, BUCKINGHAM STREET, LONDON, W.C.2.

Editors' Preface

*   *   *

The aim of this series is to provide research students and scholars with bibliographical information on aspects of Western European literature from the Middle Ages to the present day, in a convenient and accessible form. We hope to supplement, not to supplant, existing material. Single authors, periods or topics will be chosen for treatment wherever a gap needs to be filled and an authoritative scholar is prepared to fill it. Compilers will choose the form appropriate to each subject, ranging from the unannotated checklist to the selective critical bibliography; full descriptive bibliography is not, however, envisaged. Supplements will be issued, when appropriate, to keep the bibliographies up to date.

Contents

INTRODUCTION

The Exhibition organized in La Rochelle in 1970 to commemorate the 150th anniversary of the birth of Eugène Fromentin constitutes an important milestone in the field of Fromentin studies, in that there, for the first time, displayed under the same roof, were various elements drawn from all the areas of his multiplex achievement: his travel notebooks; his writings, both finished and unfinished, in the fields of literature and art criticism; his paintings, water-colours and sketches; to say nothing of the biographical elements and the voluminous correspondence. It is the aim of the present volume to offer a modest contribution to the continuation of the excellent work of the organizers of this 1970 Exhibition by compiling a bibliography of Fromentin's writings, some translations of these, and criticism relating to his work as a whole.

Faithful to the spirit in which the 1970 Exhibition was conceived, this bibliography will not attempt to establish arbitrary distinctions between the achievements of Fromentin as travel writer, painter, novelist or art critic, but will, instead, be based on the totality of his work. It is hoped that, as a result, it may be helpful not only to students concerned with these specific areas of interest, but also to those concerned with inter-subject or inter-disciplinary connections. With so ambitious an aim, the incidence of sins of omission will no doubt be the greater, though it is possible to take comfort from the fact that it is part of the policy of this series of *Research Bibliographies and Checklists* to issue supplements, when appropriate, to keep the bibliographies as complete and as up-to-date as possible. In this connection, I should be most grateful for any information which might enable me to correct errors and fill gaps.

Though, by establishing too long a list of disclaimers, one can appear to 'protest too much', the wide scope aimed at in the present bibliography calls for restrictions and qualifications. Thus, no attempt has been made to cover the following areas: Museum, Exhibition (with two exceptions, Ba7 and Ba8, where the particularly full commentaries seemed to justify the inclusion of such material in the present context), Saleroom and Bibliophiles' Catalogues; extracts from Fromentin's works which had previously been published in their entirety; entries, pertaining particularly to Fromentin's North African travels, in works published in Arabic; Encyclopaedias and general reference works relating to the history of painting or literature, where Fromentin is merely mentioned in passing. Furthermore, illustrated editions of the work of Fromentin do not appear, as such, in this bibliography, figuring only when they are accompanied by a new introduction or commentary.

This same principle of including only those editions which contain new critical comment has, in fact, been applied to the posthumous editions of the work of Fromentin in general. With regard to translations, a similar practice has been adopted: except in the case of translations into English (which are itemized in full), works translated into languages other than English have only been included where they contain new material by way of commentary or preface.

Even having established these limitations, however, there remain other areas where the aim of completeness cannot have been fulfilled. It is, for example, extremely difficult to trace all the critical accounts of Fromentin's paintings at the different Salons and Exhibitions. Again, reference has been made to translations (with commentary) of Fromentin's works into languages other than English, though here, once more, the list is doubtless incomplete; nor has any attempt been made to cover studies subsequently translated from either the French or the English original. Discourses and addresses have, where possible, been included, though omissions are inevitable in this area. With regard to newspaper articles, as also with unpublished theses and critical accounts of studies on Fromentin, it is virtually impossible to be comprehensive in coverage.

Finally, to conclude this *confiteor*, whilst, on the whole, I have limited myself to bibliographical details of those references to Fromentin which are in some degree substantial, I confess to having arbitrarily included some passing references to Fromentin which seemed to me to be particularly pertinent or to contain some new and hitherto unknown information concerning his work. Whilst scarcely satisfying the requirements of the professional bibliographer, my aim in this, as throughout the present bibliography, is to help those pursuing further research into the various aspects of Fromentin's work.

Following these principles, the bibliography, with a *terminus ad quem* of 31st July 1972, is divided in the following way:—

A: Primary Material
a: Written works published during the lifetime of Fromentin
b: Posthumous editions (including translations) with a new introduction and/or commentary
c: Correspondence and travel notes

B: Secondary Material
a: Books, periodicals, catalogues and theses wholly or substantially devoted to Fromentin
b: Articles (including less substantial parts of books etc) and references.

Items are numbered serially within these sections, thus giving cross-references of the style Aa7, Ab26, Bb137.

In Sections Aa and Ac, the order is chronological, by date of publication. The same is true, within titles, of Section Ab, where the overall order is by date of composition.

In Sections Ba and Bb, the items appear in alphabetical order by author or, in the case of a special number of a periodical or catalogue, by the title of that periodical or catalogue. Within an author, multiple items are ordered chronologically. In Section Ba, 'substantial' is taken to mean more than a quarter of any book or thesis. In this same Section, I have taken the liberty of including two theses which have not yet been presented (Ba39 and Ba40), but which, I understand, are nearing completion. Anonymous items appear, in chronological order, at the end of Section Bb.

Items in books and periodicals are presented differently:

a) Book items — Surname, forename or initials, chapter title in single quotation marks, 'in', book title in italics, place of publication: publisher, year of publication, page numbers. E.g. Bb438 Richard, Jean-Pierre, 'Paysages de Fromentin', in *Littérature et Sensation*, Paris: Seuil, 1954, pp.221 - 62.

b) Periodical item — Surname, forename or initials, article title in single quotation marks, periodical title in italics, volume in Roman numerals, issue number in Arabic numerals, date in brackets with English or numerical abbreviations (e.g. 14.11.1920 = 14th November 1920), page numbers. E.g. Bb485 Sells, A. Lytton, 'A Disciple of *Obermann*: EF', *Modern Language Review*, XXXVI, 1 (Jan. 1941), 68-85.

Minor variations on this pattern, such as the omission of a volume number, should present no serious problem.

Abbreviations are minimal and self-evident. Thus F = Fromentin, EF = Eugène Fromentin, CR = Critical review (or compte rendu), n.d. = no date, *GBA = Gazette des Beaux-Arts, RDM = Revue des Deux Mondes, NRF = Nouvelle Revue Française, PMLA = Publications of the Modern Language Association of America*. An asterisk after any entry indicates that I have not been able to check that particular item personally and have therefore relied on existing bibliographical sources for the information.

In preparing this bibliography, I have been deeply indebted to the standard bibliographies, as providing me with my principal sources of information, and most particularly, of course, to Pierre Martino's 'Fromentin: essai de bibliographie critique' (Bb329), which constitutes the only exclusively bibliographical study on Fromentin to have been published so far. In view of the special interest taken by Hector Talvart in

Introduction

Fromentin studies and his typewritten bibliographical supplement on the subject, which I have been privileged to be able to consult, the well-known *Bibliographie des auteurs modernes de langue française (1801 - 1936)* by Hector Talvart and Joseph Place must indeed take a place of pre-eminence in my acknowledgements. It should, however, be pointed out that subsequent research has failed to confirm the accuracy of some of the items of primary material listed by Talvart: the 'Vers de collégien (1838-1840)' have been itemized more specifically in Aa2; in relation to 'Notes pour une étude sur Sainte-Beuve' (see Ac1, pp.29-30) and 'Un mot sur l'art contemporain' (Ab1), claimed by Talvart to have been published in *La Charente-Inférieure* on 5th-6th July 1841, it should be stated that no issue of that newspaper appeared on the dates in question, nor did the cited articles appear in any previous or subsequent issue of *La Charente-Inférieure*; finally, despite considerable research, it has not proved possible to trace the items of art criticism by Fromentin claimed by Talvart to have been published in *L'Artiste*.

I am also indebted to Dr Roger Little who, in his earlier Saint-John Perse Bibliography for the present series, established a model which I have been happy to follow closely. My gratitude also goes to numerous friends and colleagues who have generously responded to my requests for information, notably M. Erik Dahl, the great-grandson of Fromentin, who has preserved in his home a bibliographical treasure, made available, with unfailing kindness, to all Fromentin scholars. I further owe debts to the Bibliothèque Nationale, in Paris; to the Bibliothèque Municipale, in La Rochelle; to the Library of Trinity College, Dublin; and last, but by no means least, to my publisher, Mr R. F. Cutler.

B.W.

Easter 1973.

A: PRIMARY MATERIAL

a: Written works published during the lifetime of Fromentin

Aa1 'Paraphrase du Psaume VIII', *La Charente-Inférieure*, 22 (16.3.1837), 2-3.

Aa2 Poems published in *La Charente-Inférieure*, 1838-1839:
.1 'Adieu', 99 (13.12.1838), 3.
.2 'Sommeil d'enfant', 102 (23.12.1838), 2-3.
.3 'Un Héros', 8 (27.1.1839), 3.
.4 'Chant d'espoir', 23 (21.3.1839), 3.
.5 'La Belle de nuit. Bluette', 25 (28.3.1839), 3-4.

Aa3 'Le Salon de 1845', *Revue Organique des Départements de l'Ouest*, [La Rochelle: A Caillaud] (1845), 194-208, 258-72.

Aa4 'A quoi servent les petits poètes', *ibid.*, 445-64.

Aa5 'Un Eté dans le Sahara', *Revue de Paris* (1.6.1854; 15.6.1854; 15.8.1854; 1.9.1854; 1.11.1854; 15.11.1854; 1.12.1854).

Aa6 *Un Eté dans le Sahara*, Paris: Lévy, 1857.

Aa7 'Alger. Fragments d'un journal de voyage', *L'Artiste*, LIX (July - Aug. 1857), 300-3, 321-4, 335-7.

Aa8 'Une Année dans le Sahel: Journal d'un absent', *RDM* (1.11.1858; 15.11.1858; 1.12.1858).

Aa9 *Une Année dans le Sahel*, Paris: Lévy, 1859.

Aa10 'Dominique', *RDM* (15.4.1862; 1.5.1862; 15.5.1862).

Aa11 *Dominique*, Paris: Hachette, 1863.

Aa12 Preface to 3rd edn of Aa6, Paris: Lemerre, 1874.

Aa13 'Les Maîtres d'autrefois', *RDM* (1.1.1876; 15.1.1876; 1.2.1876; 15.2.1876; 1.3.1876; 15.3.1876).

Aa14 *Les Maîtres d'autrefois: Belgique. Hollande*, Paris: Plon, 1876.

Aa15 'Chronique parisienne. Juin 1876', *Bibliothèque Universelle et Revue Suisse*, Lausanne, LVI (1876), 346-58. Anonymous article attributed to F by Pierre Blanchon, Ac2, p.404.

Aa16   'Visites artistiques, de simples pèlerinages [1852 - 1856]'. No precise source has been found for this item, or series of items, stated by Léopold Delayant, in a MS biographical note on F currently located in the Bibliothèque Municipale of La Rochelle, to have appeared in *Le Pays*. Reference to this item is nonetheless to be found in *Polybiblion*, IV (1876), 362 and in *La Grande Encyclopédie*, by Charles Grandmougin, Paris: Lamirault, [n.d.], p.203. For fuller comments and views, see Ba37, pp. 431 - 2.

b: Posthumous editions (including translations) with a new introduction and/or commentary

Ab1 'Un Mot sur l'art contemporain [: (juillet 1841)]', *GBA*, XV, 2nd period (1.4.1877), 382-5; also in Ba12, pp.15-20.

Ab2 'Une Impression de voyage' [*circa* 1841], in Bb150, pp.183-6.

Ab3 *Gustave Drouineau* (1842) [with Emile Beltrémieux], Introduction and notes by Barbara Wright, Paris: Minard, 1969, Archives des Lettres Modernes, 97.

Ab4 *Un Eté dans le Sahara*, Introduction and adaptation by B. Billioz, Paris: Société universitaire d'édition et de librairie, 1935.*

Ab5 *Un Eté dans le Sahara*, Edition expurgée à l'usage de la jeunesse, Introduction and adaptation by G. Belliot, Paris: Société universitaire d'édition et de librairie, 1936.

Ab6 *Un Eté dans le Sahara*, Introduction, commentary and notes by Maxime Revon, Paris: Conard, 1938.

Ab7 *Sahara et Sahel*, Combined edn of Aa6 and Aa9, Paris: Plon, 1877 (with re-edition in 1887).

Ab8 *Un Eté dans le Sahara, Une Année dans le Sahel*, ed. Georges Assolant, Paris: Gauthiers-Villars, 1931.

Ab9 *Dominique*, ed. Joseph Place, with bibliographical notes, Lyon: H. Lardanchet, 1920, Collection de la 'Bibliothèque du Bibliophile', Modernes.

Ab10 *Dominique*, ed. Caroline Stewart, Oxford Univ. Press, 1930, Oxford French Series.

Ab11 *Dominique*, Eng. tr. by V. I. Longman, London: Gerald Howe Ltd, 1932.

Ab12 *Dominique*, Introduction and notes by Charles Navarre, Paris: Bibliothèque Larousse, 1933.

Ab13 *Dominique*, Introduction and notes by Emile Henriot, Paris: Garnier, 1936 (with re-editions in 1955 and 1961).

Ab14 *Dominique*, Biography, commentaries and notes by Maxime Revon, Paris: Conard, 1937.

Ab15 *Dominique*, Introduction by Armand Hoog, Paris: Edns de Cluny, 1938.

Ab16 *Dominique*, Preface by Maria Sévegrand, Paris: Jacques Vautrain, 1947.

Ab17 *Dominique*, Eng. tr. by Edward Marsh, London: The Cresset Press, 1948 (repr. as a Four Square Classic, 1962, and as a NEL Signet Classic (5064), 1969).

Ab18 *Dominique*, ed. Jean Boullé, Paris: Larousse, 1952, Classiques Larousse.

Ab19 *Dominique*, Preface by Henri Mondor, Paris: A. Sauret, 1953.

Ab20 *Dominique*, Preface and notes by Henry Muller, Paris: Delmas, 1953.

Ab21 *Dominique*, Preceded by Henri Clouard, 'F' and Pierre Menanteau, '*Dominique* ou le Romantisme assagi', Paris: Edns de la Bibliothèque mondiale, 1954.

Ab22 *Dominique*, New introduction by Armand Hoog, Paris: Armand Colin, 1959, Bibliothèque de Cluny.

Ab23 *Dominique*, Introduction and notes by Barbara Wright, Oxford: Basil Blackwell, 1965, Blackwell's French Texts.

Ab24 *Dominique*, ed. Philippe Daudy, Paris: Julliard, 1965, 'Littérature', 20.

Ab25 *Dominique*, Introduction, notes etc., with the MS variants in full, by Barbara Wright, Paris: Didier, 1966, Société des Textes Français Modernes, 2 vols.

Ab26 *Dominique*, Preface by André Fraigneau, notes etc., by Samuel Silvestre de Sacy, Paris: Le Livre de poche, 1966.

Ab27 *Dominique*, Preface by Roger Denux, Paris: La Fenêtre Ouverte, 1967.

Ab28 *Dominique*, Introduction etc., by Guy Sagnes, Paris: Garnier-Flammarion, 1967.

Ab29 *Dominique*, Avant-propos de l'éditeur, [Paris] : Jules Tallandier, 1967.

Ab30 *Dominique*, German tr. by Ferdinand Hardekopf, Postface by Ernst Howald, Zurich: Manesse Verlag, Conzett & Huber, 1967.

Ab31 *Dominique*, Foreword by Jeanlouis Cornuz, Lausanne: Edns Rencontre, 1968.

Ab32 *Dominique*, Roumanian tr. by Toma Vlădescu, Bucharest: Editura pentru literatură, 1968.*

Ab32a *Dominique*, Italian tr. by Rosetta Loy Provera, Preface by Roland Barthes, Turin: Einaudi, 1972.*

Ab33 *Dominique*, Morceaux choisis, Presented by John W. Batchelor, Paris: Didier, 1969, Les Classiques de la Civilisation Française.

Ab34 'L'Ile de Ré' (fragment) (1862), in Ba12, pp.341-55.

Ab35 'Un Programme de critique' (1864?), in Ba12, pp.105-24.

Ab36 'Voyage en Egypte' (1869), in Ba12, pp.257-339.

Ab37 *Voyage en Egypte (1869)*, Journal publié d'après le carnet manuscrit, Introduction and notes by Jean-Marie Carré, Paris: Fernand Aubier, 1935, Edns Montaigne.

Ab38 Wright, Barbara, 'Un Poème inédit de F: *La Fin du Rhamadan*' (1874), *French Review*, XXXVIII, 6 (May 1965), 777-80.

Ab39 *The Old Masters of Belgium and Holland*, Eng. tr. by Mary C. Robbins, Boston & New York: Houghton Mifflin Co., 1882, and Boston: J. R. Osgood & Co., 1882.* (Repr., New York: Schocken, 1964.)

Ab40 *Les Maîtres d'autrefois*, ed. H. Peyre de Betouzet, Paris: Hatier, 1932, Collection 'Les Classiques pour tous'.

Ab41 *Les Maîtres d'autrefois*, Preface, notes etc., by Maurice Allemand, Paris: Garnier, 1939.

Ab42 *I maestri d'un tempo*, Ital. tr. by Anna Bovero, preface by Mary Pittaluga, Borius, F. De Silva, 1943.*

Ab43 *Les Plus Belles Pages consacrées à Pierre-Paul Rubens par EF dans les 'Maîtres d'Autrefois'*, Collected and annotated by Armand Davesnes, Brussels: Office de publicité, 1944.

Ab44 *Les Maîtres d'autrefois. Belgique-Hollande*, Annotated by Willy Rotzler, Bâle: Edns Holbein, [1947].*

Ab45 *Les Maîtres d'autrefois*, Introduction by André Lhote, Brussels: L'Ecran du Monde, & Paris: Les Deux Sirènes, 1948.

Ab46 *The Masters of Past Time*, Eng. tr. by Andrew Boyle, Introduction and notes by H. Gerson, London: Phaidon Press, 1948.

Ab47 *De oude meesters [Les Maîtres d'autrefois]* Dutch tr. by J. Tersteeg, Rijswijk: Leidsche U.M., 1950.*

Ab48 *De meesters van weleer*, Dutch tr., with introduction, notes etc., by H. Van de Waal, Rotterdam: Ad. Donker, 1951.

Ab49 *Mistrzowie dawni [Les Maîtres d'autrefois]*, Polish tr., by Jan Cybis, Wroclaw: Zaklad im. Ossolinskieh, 1956.*

Ab50 *Stari mistri*, Czech tr. by Dagmar Mala, Followed by Jaromir Neumann, 'O literarnim dile EF', and notes etc. by Bohumir Mraz, Prague: Statni nakladatelstvi krasne literatury, hudby a umeni, 1957.

Ab51   *Les Maîtres d'autrefois*, Presented and annotated by Jacques Foucart, Paris: Le Livre de poche, 1965.

Ab52   *Les Maîtres d'autrefois*, Introduction, notes etc., with MS variants, by Pierre Moisy, Paris: Garnier, 1972.

Ab53   *Textes choisis de F*, Introduction by Maxime Revon, Bruges: Desclée de Brouwer et Cie, 1936.

c: Correspondence and travel notes

Ac1   *EF, Lettres de jeunesse*, Biography and notes by Pierre Blanchon, Paris: Plon, 1909.
This work incorporates the letters appearing in the following earlier publications:

  .1   'Deux lettres inédites de F', *Revue des Charentes* (30.9.1905), 24-6.

  .2   Jacques-André Mérys (pseudonym of Pierre Blanchon), 'Lettres de jeunesse de F (1847, 1848)', *RDM*, XXIX (1905), 578-619.

  .3   Pierre Blanchon, 'La Jeunesse d'EF', *Revue Hebdomadaire* (2.1.1909), 77-101.

  .4   Pierre Blanchon, 'La Révélation de l'Orient', *Revue Bleue* (24.10.1908), 513-19;   (31.10.1908), 548-54.

Ac2   *EF, Correspondance et fragments inédits*, Biography and notes by Pierre Blanchon, Paris: Plon, 1912.
This work incorporates the letters appearing in the following earlier publications:

  .1   'EF, Lettres de voyage en Belgique et en Hollande', *RDM* (15.7.1908), 241-83.

  .2   'EF, Lettres et fragments inédits (1848-1876)', *RDM* (1.2.1912), 581-612.

  .3   'EF, Lettres inédites', *Le Temps* (1.2.1912).

  .4   'EF, Lettres inédites', *La Revue (Ancienne 'Revue des Revues')* (15.2.1912), 479-92.

Ac3   Fromentin-George Sand correspondence:

  .1   Ba12, pp.143-56, 158-71.

  .2   Pierre Blanchon, 'Lettres de George Sand à EF', *Revue de Paris*, XVIII (15.9.1909), 258-82; XIX (1.10.1909), 531-46.

  .3   Ac2, pp.93-100, 109-19, 124-6, 136-78 and *passim*.

  .4   Ab25, vol. II, pp.487-98.

Ac4   Travel notes of Fromentin during his visit to the Low Countries published by Pierre Blanchon as follows:

  .1   'Les Peintres hollandais', *Revue de Paris* (1.7.1911), 5-35; (15.7.1911), 301-16.

  .2   'Les Peintres flamands', *ibid.*, (15.1.1912), 225-50; (1.2.1912), 623-47.

Ac5   'Quelques lettres inédites d'EF' (Commentary by Pierre Blanchon), in Ba18, pp.2-17. To his mother (26.10.1846); to his parents (22.1.1847); to Emile Beltrémieux (4.5.1847); to his mother (4.9.1847); to Gaston Romieux (Spring 1858); to Charles Busson (29.9.1866); to Alexandre Protais (28.11.1870).

Ac6　'Lettres inédites de F, locataire à Diaz, propriétaire', *La Renaissance Politique, Littéraire, Artistique* (30.10.1920), 3-4. To Narcisse Diaz (12.10.1865; 7.11.1865; 15.1.1866; 13.10.1868; 27.3.1871; 5.7.1871; 19.10.1871; March 1872).

Ac7　'Trois lettres inédites d'EF', in Ba16. To Armand du Mesnil (Aug. 1851); to Paul Bataillard (25.5.1859); to Alexandre Bida (17.8.1869).

Ac8　'Un Curieux Document sur deux ouvrages de F' (Extrait d'une lettre d'EF à l'imprimeur Claye), 'Echos', *Bulletin du Bibliophile* (March 1927), 141.

Ac9　To Gustave Flaubert, in Bb10, pp.143-4.

Ac10　To Lilia Beltrémieux (19.7.[1869]), in *Dominique*, Paris: Edns Richard, 1929.

Ac11　To Léopold Delayant (19.4.1856), in Bb404. A facsimile of this letter appears in *Annales de l'Académie des Belles-Lettres et Arts de La Rochelle*, 1930.

Ac12　Gambier, P. 'Un ami de F: Félix Sainton', *Revue du Bas-Poitou*, LXVII (April 1956), 107-16. To Félix Sainton (2.5.[1840]) (publ. in part, Ac1, p.39); 5.12.[1857]; 15.7.1859; [Sept. 1859?]; 15.8.1862; 20.1.[1868]; 27.5.1868; 4.6.1873). See also Bb202.

Ac13　Wright, Barbara & Moisy, Pierre, *Gustave Moreau et EF: Documents inédits*, with introduction, notes etc., La Rochelle: Quartier Latin, 1972.

Notes

Notes

B: SECONDARY MATERIAL

a: Books, periodicals, catalogues and theses wholly or substantially devoted to Fromentin

Ba1   *Académie de La Rochelle, Séances Publiques de 1929 à 1932,* La Rochelle, 1933. Discours de Hector Talvart (pp.49-50), André Demaison (pp.51-6), Pierre Blanchon (pp.56-64), Gaston Picard (pp.64-9).
Les Arts: see Ba19.

Ba2   Beaume, Georges, *F*, Paris: Louis Michaud, [n.d.].

Ba3   Brard, Ernest, *Nos gloires nationales. EF*, La Rochelle: Imprimerie Masson et Cie, 1902. Reprint of Bb82.

Ba4   Burty, Philippe, *25 dessins d'EF reproduits à l'eau-forte par E. L. Montefiore*, Paris-London: Librairie de l'art, 1877.

Ba5   Dorbec, Prosper, *EF: Biographie critique*, Paris: Laurens, 1926.

Ba6   Eckstein, Marie-Anne, *Le rôle du souvenir dans l'oeuvre d'EF*, Thesis presented to Univ. of Zurich, Zurich: Juris-Verlag, 1970.

Ba7   *EF, le peintre et l'écrivain, 1820-1876*, Catalogue de l'Exposition en 1970 à la Bibliothèque Municipale et au Musée des Beaux-Arts de La Rochelle, La Rochelle, 1970. Notices rédigées par Olga de Saint-Affrique, Carmen Montibert-Ducros et Lise Carrier; Avant-Propos d'André Salardaine.
This work further incorporates Bb355, 369, 564.

Ba8   *EF, Pierre Loti et la tradition d'exotisme en Poitou et en Charentes aux XIXe et XXe siècles*, Catalogue de l'Exposition de Pâques 1954 au Musée de Poitiers, à l'occasion du centenaire de 'Un Eté dans le Sahara' (4.4.1954 – 2.5.1954), Catalogue by Marc Sandoz, Poitiers: Société des Amis des Musées de Poitiers, 1954.

Ba9   Evans, Arthur Robert (Jr), *The Literary Art of EF: A Study in Style and Motif* (Thesis presented to Univ. of Minnesota, 1960), Baltimore: The Johns Hopkins Press, 1964.
Le Figaro: see Ba16.

Ba10   Gaudin, Paul, *Essai sur EF*, La Rochelle: Siret, 1877.

Ba11   Giraud, Victor, *EF*, Niort: Edns Saint-Denis, 1945. Reprint of Bb241.

Ba12   Gonse, Louis, *EF, peintre et écrivain*, Paris: Quantin, 1881. Reprint of Bb251. See Ab34, 35, 36; Ac3.1.

Ba13   Kappeler, Waltrud, *F, ein Dichter der Erinnerung*, Thesis presented to Univ. of Zurich, Winterthur-Töss: Buchdruckerie Paul Gehring, 1949

Ba14   Lagrange, Andrée, *L'Art de F*, Paris: Edns Dervy, 1952.

Ba15   *La Libre Parole* (20.5.1921; 24.5.1921; 27.5.1921), 'L'Illustration de *Dominique*' incorporating Bb152 and:
 .1   'Le Roman de F et l'idée de René Helleu' (24.5.1921).
 .2   'Le Pèlerinage de Jean Perrier' (27.5.1921).

Ba16   *Le Figaro. Supplément littéraire du samedi* (28.8.1926). This issue incorporates Ac7; Bb70, 196, 402.

Ba17   Lehtonen, Maija, 'Essai sur *Dominique* de F' *Annales Academiae Scientiarum Fennicae*, Ser. B, CLXXVI, Helsinki, Suomalainen Tiedeakatemia, 1972.

Ba18   *Le Pays d'Ouest. Revue des Charentes et du Poitou* (Oct. 1920). This issue incorporates Ac5; Bb115, 272, 493, 520 and:
 .1   'Une Page du manuscrit de *Dominique*', 18-19.

Ba19   *Les Arts*, CIV (1910). *

  La Libre Parole: see Ba15.

Ba20   Magowan, Robin, 'The Art of Pastoral Narrative: Sand, F, Jewett', Thesis presented to Yale Univ., 1963-4.*

Ba21   Montibert-Ducros, Carmen, 'Essai de Catalogue d'EF, 1820-1876', Mémoire, Ecole du Louvre, 1970.

Ba22   Morcos, Fouad, 'F et l'Afrique: Algérie – Egypte', Thesis presented to Univ. of Paris, 1954.

Ba23   *North American Review*, 'Contemporary French Literature', LXXXVI (Jan. 1858), 219-42; LXXXIX (July 1859), 209-32.

Ba24   Ollivier, A., *EF peintre et écrivain*, La Rochelle: Imprimerie Rochelaise, [1903].

Ba25   Osaji, Fidelis Chukwudebe, 'Le Sentiment de la nature dans *Dominique* d'EF', Master's thesis presented to Laval Univ., Quebec, 1968.*

Ba26   Otten-Niederer, E. J. M., 'L'Oeil de F avant *Les Maîtres d'autrefois*', Thesis presented to Univ. of Nijmegen, 1964.*

Le Pays d'Ouest: see Ba18

Ba27   Pellegrini, Carlo, *EF, scrittore*, Ferrara: Taddei, 1921.

Ba28   Philouze, Léon, *EF*, Vannes: Imprimerie Lafolye, 1898.

Ba29   Ramses, Ishak, 'Le Vocabulaire psychologique de F dans *Dominique*', Thesis presented to Univ. of Paris, 1951.

Ba30   *Revue des Charentes* (30.9.1905).
        This issue incorporates Ac1.1; Bb20, 67, 187, 237, 491, 525 and:
    .1 Brunetière, Ferdinand, 'Extraits de la conférence du 29 octobre 1903 à La Rochelle', 5-8.
    .2 Dupont, Léonce, 'Le Triomphe (poème)', 73-74.
    .3 'Extraits critiques de Sainte-Beuve, George Sand, Ernest Chesneau, Jules Breton', 75-79.
    .4 'Enquête artistique et littéraire sur F (Réponses de Jules Clarétie, Arvède Barine, Maurice Barrès, Gaston Deschamps, Louis Gonse, Joachim Merlant, Charles Saunier)', 80-86.
    .5 'Bibliographie', 87.

Ba31   *Revue du Bas-Poitou et des Provinces de l'Ouest*, LXXXI, 3 (May - June 1970).
        This issue incorporates Bb78, 102, 142, 300, 355, 362, 369, 458, 466, 564 and:
    .1 'Bibliographie sommaire', 101-2.

Ba32   Reynaud, Camille, *La Genèse de 'Dominique'*, Grenoble: Arthaud, 1937. Repr. of Bb436.

Ba33   Roujon, Henry (Coll. 'Les Peintres illustres' directed by), *F*, Paris: Lafitte, [1912].

Ba34   Thibaudet, Albert, 'F', in *Intérieurs*, Paris: Plon, 1924. Repr. of Bb521.

Ba35   Tranmer, Elsie, 'EF, his life and work', M.A. thesis, Univ. of Birmingham, 1921.

Ba36   Vier, Jacques, *Pour l'étude du 'Dominique' de F*, Paris: Minard, 1958, Archives des Lettres Modernes, 16-17. Repr. of Bb539, 540.

Ba37   Wright, Barbara, 'A Critical Analysis of *Dominique*, with particular reference to the manuscript and other works of EF (1820-1876)', Ph.D. thesis, Univ. of Cambridge, 1962.

Ba38   Zimmermans, Hela, 'EF, Leben, Kunst und Kunstauffassung', Thesis presented to Univ. of Heidelberg, 1943.*

Ba39   Christin, Anne-Marie, 'F ou les métaphores du refus: Les récits algériens et leur genèse', Thesis for presentation to Univ. of Paris IV, In preparation.

Ba40   Mellors, Terence, 'Aesthetic Perception and Expression in F', Thesis for presentation to Univ. of Oxford, In preparation.

b: Articles (including less substantial parts of books etc.) and references

Bb1   Abbes, Paul d', 'Le Centenaire de F', *Le Monde Illustré* (16.10.1920).

Bb2   About, Edmond, 'Le Salon de 1857', *Le Moniteur Universel* (5.9.1857).

Bb3   —, 'Le Salon de 1868', *RDM* (1.6.1868).

Bb4   Abraham, Pierre, in *Figures*, Paris: NRF, 1929, pp.80-3.

Bb5   Alain-Fournier, 'Portrait', in *Miracles*, Paris: NRF, 1924, pp.204-5. See also Bb441.

Bb6   Alazard, Jean, Refs in *L'Orient et la peinture française au XIXe siècle, d'Eugène Delacroix à Auguste Renoir*, Paris: Plon, 1930, Ch.VII, Ch.VIII & *passim*.

Bb7   —, 'Comment F a vu l'Afrique du Nord', *Le Correspondant* (25.4.1930), 243-59.

Bb8   —, 'Les Peintres de l'Algérie au XIXe siècle', *GBA* (June 1930), 370-87.

Bb9   —, 'L'Algérie et les arts de 1830 à nos jours', in *Histoire et Historiens de l'Algérie*, Paris: Félix Alcan, 1931, pp.349-62.

Bb10   Albalat, Antoine, in *Gustave Flaubert et ses amis*, Paris: Plon, 1927, pp.143-4. See also Ac9.

Bb11   Alexandre, Arsène, 'Artistes qui écrivirent. F et *Les Maîtres d'autrefois*', *Les Nouvelles Littéraires* (6.2.1932).

Bb12   Alix, 'Les Grands Artistes de France: F', *Petit Echo de la Mode* (20.2.1927).

         Allemand, Maurice: see Ab41.

Bb13   Ambrière, Francis, 'Peintre ou romancier? ', *Les Nouvelles Littéraires* (4.3.1939).

Bb14   Arès, 'F', *La Gazette de France* (3.10.1905).

Bb15   Arland, Marcel, '*Dominique* et F', *La Nef* (June 1945), 18-32; reprinted in *Les Echanges*, Paris: Gallimard, 1946, pp.205-29.

Bb16   Arnauldet, Thomas, 'Les Artistes bretons, angevins et poitevins au Salon de 1857', *Revue des Provinces de l'Ouest*, Nantes (1857).*

Bb17   Arnould, E.J., CR of Ab23 and Ab25, *Hermathena*, CIV (Spring 1967), 85-7.

Assolant, Georges: see Ab8

Bb18 Aubecourt, E. d', 'EF, peintre et écrivain', *Polybiblion*, XXXII (1881), 514-5.

Bb19 Aubray, Gabriel, 'Causerie littéraire. A propos du monument de F. L'enfance de Dominique', *Le Mois Littéraire et Pittoresque* (Oct. 1903), 484-94.

Bb20 Audiat, Gabriel, *'Dominique'*, in Ba30, pp.34-52.

Bb21 Audibert, Raoul, 'Les Travaux et les jours de Dominique', *Les Nouvelles Littéraires* (19.4.1962), 6.

Bb22 Avit, R., 'Le 150e anniversaire de la naissance d'EF. Deux expositions font revivre l'écrivain et le peintre dans son époque', *Le Sud-Ouest* (1.6.1970).

Bb23 —, 'Tout savoir sur EF. Le peintre et l'écrivain. Sa vie et son temps, à la Bibliothèque Municipale [de La Rochelle]', *Le Sud-Ouest* (18.7.1970; 20.7.1970).

Bb24 B, H., 'George Sand critique', *Journal des Débats* (1.10.1909), 642-3.

Bb25 B, J., 'Le Centenaire de F', *Le Temps* (15.9.1920).

Bb26 Bachelard, Gaston, Ref. in *La Poétique de la rêverie*, Paris: Presses Universitaires de France, 1965, p.21.

Bb27 Baignières, Arthur, 'Revue artistique. Exposition des œuvres d'EF à l'Ecole nationale des Beaux-Arts', *Journal Officiel* (21.3.1877).

Bb28 Baille, Frédéric, 'M. EF, candidat à l'Académie française', *La Revue de France*, XVIII (May 1876), 639-43.

Bb29 Bangor, E.-G., 'EF, peintre et littérateur (1820-1876)', *Les Contemporains* (Dec. 1905), 1-16.

Bb30 Banville, Théodore de, 'Le Salon de 1861', *Revue Fantaisiste* (15.5.1861), 38-41.

Bb31 Barberey, Bernard, 'EF', *L'Olivier, Revue de Nice* (May 1913), 275-86; (June 1913), 367-81.

Bb32 Barbéris, Pierre, in *Balzac et le mal du siècle*, Paris: Gallimard, 1970, vol. II, pp.1856-9.

Bb33 Barbey d'Aurévilly, Jules-Amédée, ['EF'], *Le Pays* (17.5.1859); reprinted in *Voyageurs er romanciers*, Paris: Lemerre, 1908, pp.105-9.

Bb34 —, 'Un Homme plus grand que son fauteuil', *Le Triboulet* (25.12.1880).

Barine, Arvède: see Ba30.4

Bb35 Barneville, Pierre de, in *Au seuil du siècle*, Paris: Perrin, 1902, pp.250-1.

Bb36 Barrère, Jean-Bertrand, Refs in *L'Idée du goût, de Pascal à Valéry*, Paris: Klincksieck, 1972, Collection Critères, pp.101, 103, 170, 178.

Bb37 Barrès, Maurice, 'Mes Cahiers' in *L'Œuvre de Maurice Barrès*, annotated by Philippe Barrès, Paris: Au Club de l'Honnête Homme, 1968, vol. XIV, p.95; vol. XVII, p.44. See also Ba30.4.

Bb37a Barthes, Roland, 'F: *Dominique*' [repr. of preface to Ab32a], in *Le Degré zéro de l'écriture, suivi de Nouveaux essais critiques*, Paris: Seuil, 1972, Coll. Points, pp.156-69.

Bb38 Barthou, Louis, in *'Pêcheur d'Islande' de Pierre Loti. Etude et analyse*, Paris: Mellotée, 1929, pp.271, 326-7.

Batchelor, John W.: see Ab33.

Bb39 Baudelaire, Charles, in *Œuvres complètes*, Paris: Gallimard, 1954, Bibl. de la Pléiade, pp.235, 763, 789, 801-3, 819, 1278.

Bb40 —, *Correspondance générale*, ed. Jacques Crépet, Paris: Conard, 1947, vol.II, p.114.

Bb41 Bazin, René, 'Un Peintre écrivain: F', *Revue Bleue* (24.4.1897), 513-7; (1.5.1897), 549-54; repr. in *Questions littéraires et sociales*, Paris: Calmann-Lévy, 1906, pp.1-37.

Bb42 —, 'L'Œuvre littéraire d'EF', *Annales Politiques et Littéraires* (1.10.1905), 219-21; (8.10.1905), 234-6.

Bb43 Beaume, Georges, 'Les F', *La France de Bordeaux et du Sud-Ouest* (1.1.1933).

Bb44 —, 'Dominique', *La France de Bordeaux et du Sud-Ouest* (8.4.1933).

Bb45 Bellaigue, Camille, 'EF', *Le Correspondant* (25.7.1891), 309-37; repr. in *Impressions musicales et littéraires*, Paris: Delagrave, 1900, pp.385-449.

Bb46 Bellessort, André, 'Réflexions sur F à propos de son centenaire', *Le Correspondant* (25.10.1920), 217-35; repr. in *Nouvelles Etudes et autres figures*, Paris: Bloud et Gay, 1923, pp.175-202.

Belliot, G.: see Ab5.

Bb47 Benson, Eugene, 'EF', *The Galaxy* (15.11.1866), 533-8.

Bb48 Bergerat, Emile, 'EF', *Journal Officiel de la République Française* (14.10.1876).

Bb49   —, 'Notes sur EF', *ibid.* (28.1.1877).

Bb50   Berki, N., ''Rembrandt d'après F', *Budapesti Szemle* (Oct. 1906).*

Bb51   Bernard, Daniel, 'Variétés: *Un Eté dans le Sahara – Une Année dans le Sahel'*, *L'Union* (17.9.1874).

Bb52   Bersaucourt, Albert de, 'F et la critique', *Revue Critique des Idées et des Livres*, XXX (25.11.1920), 464-6.

Bb53   Berthelot, Paul, 'F' in *Artistes contemporains des pays de Guyenne. Béarn, Saintonge et Languedoc*, Bordeaux: Gounouilhou, 1889, pp.65-74.

Bb54   Białostocki, Jan, 'Miedzy Romantyzmem a Pozytywizmem. Stanowisko Fromentina w dziejach krytyki artystycznej', *Materiałów do studiów i dyskusji z zakresu teorii i historii sztuki, krytyki artystycznej oraz badan nad sztuka*, Panstwowy Instytut Sztuki, I, 17 (1954), 160-208.

Bb55   Bigot, Charles, 'Causerie Artistique', *Revue Politique et Littéraire (Revue Bleue)*, XI (15.7.1876), 61-2.

Bb56   —, ['EF'], *Revue Politique et Littéraire (Revue Bleue)*, XII (14.4.1877), 989-95; repr. in *Peintres français contemporains*, Paris: Hachette, 1888, pp.77-102.

       Billioz, B.: see Ab4

Bb57   Billy, André, 'Le Centenaire de F', *L'Opinion* (2.10.1920).

Bb58   —, 'Les Propos du samedi', *Le Figaro Littéraire* (28.9.1963; 7/13.11.1963).

Bb59   —, 'Propos', *Le Figaro Littéraire* (16.2.1967).

Bb60   Blanc, Charles, 'Le Salon de 1866', *GBA*, XXI (1.7.1866), 40-1.

Bb61   —, 'EF: A Paul de Saint-Victor', *Le Moniteur Universel* (5.9.1876); repr. in *L'Artiste* (1.11.1876), 287-94.

Bb62   —, 'Lettres de Hollande', *Le Temps* (5.10.1876; 11.10.1876).

Bb63   Blanche, Jacques-Emile, Refs in *Propos de Peintre: De David à Degas*, Ser. I, Paris: Emile-Paul [4th edn], 1919, pp.168, 302. See also Bb422.

Bb64   —, Ref. in *Hommage à André Gide*, Paris: Edns du Capitole, 1928, p.102.

Bb65   —, Refs in *Les Arts plastiques*, Paris: Les Edns de France, 1931, pp.6, 8, 92, 134, 135.

Bb66   Blanchon, Pierre [see also Ac1, 2, 3.2, 4, 5; Ba1], 'EF écrivain', *Journal des Débats* (31.12.1902).

Bb67   —, 'F: sa vie (d'après des documents inédits)', in Ba30, pp.11-23.

Bb68   —, 'L'Originalité de *Dominique*', *Revue Bleue* (5.6.1909), 726-8; (12.6.1909), 754-9.

Bb69   —, 'Au jour le jour: A propos d'une lettre d'EF', *Journal des Débats* (20.2.1920).

Bb70   —, 'La Vie et l'œuvre d'EF', in Ba16.

Bb71   —, ['EF'], 2 lectures given to the Section des Belles-Lettres de l'Académie de la Rochelle (5.11.1926; 15.11.1926).

Bb72   —, 'Quelle fut la Madeleine de Dominique? ', *Le Figaro* (9.6.1928).

Bb73   —, *'Le Voyage en Egypte* d'EF', *La Charente-Inférieure* (12.11.1935).

Bb74   —, 'Le Style de F d'après ses manuscrits', *Annales de l'Académie de La Rochelle: Section des Belles-Lettres et des Beaux-Arts* (1936), 58-75.

Bb75   Bloch, Vitale, 'F e sui *Maîtres d'autrefois*', *Paragone* (1950), 24-8.

Bb76   —, 'A propos d'une réédition du Livre de poche: EF, *Les Maîtres d'autrefois*' [review article based on Ab51], *L'Information d'Histoire de l'Art*, XII, 4 (Sept.-Oct. 1967), 183-6

Bb77   Bonnin, A., 'Salon de 1876', *L'Art*, VI (1876), 22.

Bb78   Bonniot, Roger, 'EF et Gustave Courbet', in Ba31, pp.65-6.

Bb79   Bordeaux, Henry, ['EF'], *Revue Hebdomadaire* (22.12.1900), 561-72; repr. in *Les Ecrivains et les mœurs*, Ser. II, Paris: Plon, 1902, pp.58-69.

Bb80   Bornecque, Jacques-Henry, Refs in *Les Années d'apprentissage d'Alphonse Daudet*, Paris: Nizet, 1951, pp.330, 338, 343, 362, 515.

Bb81   Bou, Gilbert, Refs in *Quatorze tableaux de Gustave Moreau: Le Chemin de Croix de l'Eglise Notre-Dame de Decazeville*, Rodez: Edns Subervie, 1964, pp.16, 17 n.1.

        Boullé, Jean: see Ab18.

Bb82   Brard, Ernest, 'Nos gloires nationales: EF', *Courrier de La Rochelle* (30.10.1902); repr. in Ba3.

Bb83   Bremner, Geoffrey, 'Ambivalence in *Dominique*', *Forum for Modern Language Studies*, V (1969), 323-30.

Bb84   Breton, Jules, in *La Vie d'un artiste*, Paris: Lemerre, 1890, pp.319-21.

Bb85   ——, in *Un Peintre paysan: souvenirs et impressions*, Paris: Lemerre, 1895, pp.287-8.

Bb86   ——, in *Nos peintres du siècle: l'art et les artistes*, Paris: Société d'édn artistique, [1899], pp.139-45, 178.

Bb87   Briquet, Pierre-E., Refs in *Pierre Loti et l'Orient*, Geneva: Imprimerie du 'Journal de Genève', 1945, pp.101-2; 286-7.

Bb88   Bruller, Jean, '*Dominique*', *La Quinzaine Critique* (25.12.1929), 198-9.

Bb89   Brunetière, Ferdinand, 'EF et la critique d'art', *Le Correspondant* (10.10.1903), 67-84; repr. in *Variétés littéraires*, Paris: Calmann-Lévy, 1904, pp.243-76. See also Ba30.1.

Bb90   Bürger, W., *Salons, 1861 à 1868*, Paris: Renouard, 1870, vol. I, p.385; vol. II, p.311.*

Bb91   C, C., CR of Ac2, *Polybiblion*, Ser. II, LXXVII (1912).

Bb92   Cadars, Pierre, in *Les Débuts de Gustave Moreau (1848-1864)*, Thesis presented to Univ. of Toulouse, 1965, pp.1, 46-66, 78, 80-2, 84, 88, 90, 108.

Bb93   Callias, Hector de, 'Le Salon de 1861', [VIII], *L'Artiste* [n.s.], XII (15.6.1861), 267.

Bb94   Calvet, Jean, Refs in *Le Renouveau catholique dans la littérature contemporaine*, Paris: F. Lanore, 1931, pp.109-10, 116.

Bb95   Cantrel, E., 'Salon de 1863', *L'Artiste*, V (1.5.1863), 195.*

Bb96   Capus, Alfred, Ref. in *Monsieur Piégeois*, Comédie en 3 actes, Paris: Imprimerie de 'l'Illustration', 1905, pp.26-7.

Bb97   Carré, Jean-Marie, in *Voyageurs et écrivains français en Egypte (1517-1869)*, Cairo: Edns de l'Institut français d'archéologie orientale, 1933, vol. II, pp.319-42. See also Ab37.

       Carrier, Lise: see Ba7.

Bb98   Cassagne, Albert, Refs in *La Théorie de l'art pour l'art en France, chez les derniers romantiques et les premiers réalistes*, Paris: Lucien Dorbon, 1959, [repr. of 1905 edn], pp.76, 98, 110, 127, 135, 138, 162, 187, 300-1, 303, 349, 361, 368, 370-1, 376, 378.

Bb99 Castagnary, Jules, 'Salon de 1861', in *Les Artistes au XIXe siècle*, Paris: Librairie Nouvelle, [n.d.], pp.25-7.

Bb100 Castex, Pierre-Georges, 'F', in *La Critique d'art en France au XIXe siècle*, Paris: Centre de Documentation Universitaire, 1958, vol. II, pp.117-40.

Bb101 Chadourne, Louis, Ref. in *L'Inquiète Adolescence*, Paris: Albin Michel, 1920, pp.138-9.

Bb102 Chaigne, Louis, 'Hommage à EF', in Ba31, pp.3-4.

Bb103 Chalon, Louis, 'Du rythme au poème: Analyse d'une page de F' [*Dominique*, 'Quelques minutes seulement . ', Ab13, p.79], *Cahiers d'Analyse Textuelle*, V (1963), 51-60.

Bb104 —, 'Analyse d'une page de F' [*Dominique*, 'L'absence a des effets singuliers . . .', Ab13, p.16], *Cahiers d'Analyse Textuelle*, VIII (1966), 61-9.

Bb105 —, 'EF: Le silence saharien', *Cahiers d'Analyse Textuelle*, XII (1970), 49-56.

Bb106 Chardonne, Jacques, Ref. in *Matinales*, Paris: Albin Michel, p.17.

Bb107 Charles, Etienne, 'Le Centenaire de F', *Revue de la Semaine* (12.11.1920), 119-20.

Bb108 Charlton, D.G., 'F's *Dominique*' [review article based on Ab23], *Forum for Modern Language Studies*, III (1967), 85-92.

Bb109 Charnage, D. de, 'Musées de province: La Rochelle et F', *La Croix* (15.9.1931).

Bb110 Chastel, André, 'Au Musée et à la Bibliothèque de La Rochelle: L'émouvant souvenir de F', *Le Monde* (6.8.1970).

Bb111 Chaumelin, Marius, 'Salon de 1868' in *L'Art contemporain*, Paris: Renouard, 1873, pp.112-3, 126, 154, 181.

Bb112 Cherbuliez, Victor, 'Le Salon de 1876', [II], *RDM*, XV (15.6.1876).

Bb113 Chernowitz, Maurice E., Refs in *Proust and Painting*, New York: International Univ. Press, 1945, *passim*.

Bb114 Chesneau, Ernest, in *Les Nations rivales dans l'art*, Paris: Didier, 1868, pp.312-6; 348-50.

Bb115 Chevrillon, André, 'L'Art de F dans ses livres sur l'Algérie', in Ba18, pp.20-6.

Bb116 —, 'Sur les pas de F', *Revue Européenne* (15.5.1927), 369-91.

Bb117 Clarétie, Jules, 'Peintres et sculpteurs contemporains', *L'Artiste* (1.3.1864); repr., under same title, Paris: Charpentier, 1873, pp.41-5 & *passim*. See also Ba30.4.

Bb118 Claudel, Paul, in *Œuvres en prose*, Paris: Gallimard, 1965, Edns de la Pléiade, pp.25, 175-7, 194, 199, 647.

Bb119 Clément, Charles, 'Variétés: L'atelier d'EF', *Journal des Débats* (26.1.1877).

Bb120 Clément de Ris, L., 'Le Salon de 1851', *L'Artiste* (1.2.1851), 8.

Bb121 —, 'Le Salon de 1853', *L'Artiste* (15.7.1853), 180.

Bb122 —, 'Les Notabilités de l'art depuis dix ans', *L'Artiste* (27.6.1858), 116-22.

Bb123 Clément-Janin, 'A propos de *Dominique*', *Candide* (22.5.1930).

Clouard, Henri: see Ab21.

Bb124 Cocking, J. M., Ref. in *Proust*, London: Bowes & Bowes, 1956, pp.27-8.

Bb125 Compton, C. G., 'EF', *The Fortnightly Review*, LXXXIII [old ser.] (1905), 508-19.

Bb126 Comte, Jules, 'EF', *L'Illustration* (9.9.1876).

Bb127 Coquelin, Louis, CR of Ac1, *Larousse Mensuel Illustré*, XXVII (May 1909), 461-2.

Bb128 Cormary, H., '*Dominique* d'EF: roman de l'Aunis – roman du souvenir', lecture given to the Cercle de la Maison de la Glycine, Rochefort (20.1.1932).

Cornuz, Jeanlouis: see Ab31.

Bb129 Courthion, Pierre, 'EF, critique d'art et esthète', *Revue Hebdomadaire*, X (23.10.1926), 477-86.

Bb130 Cressot, Marcel, 'Le Sens de *Dominique*', *Revue d'Histoire Littéraire de la France* (Apr. - June 1928), 211-8.

Bb131 Croce, Benedetto, Ref. in *Nuovi Saggi di Estetica*, Bari: Gius, Laterza & Figli, 1926, p.268.

Bb132 —, Ref. in *Ultimi Saggi*, Bari: Gius, Laterza & Figli, 1935, p.190.

Bb133 Crouzet, Marcel, in *Un Méconnu du réalisme: Duranty (1833-1880)*, Paris: Nizet, 1964, pp.261, 288, 311, 322, 342, 379.

Bb134 Cruickshank, John, 'The Novel of Self-Disclosure', in *French Literature and its Background*: IV, *The Early Nineteenth Century*, London, Oxford, New York: Oxford Univ. Press, 1969, pp. 170-88.

Bb135   Cuvillier-Fleury, Alfred-Auguste, 'Voyages et voyageurs',
         Journal des Débats (27.5.1860); repr. in *Historiens, poètes
         et romanciers*, Paris: Lévy, 1863, vol.II, pp.267-8.

Bb136   Czoniczer, Elisabeth, in *Quelques antécédents de 'A la
         recherche du temps perdu'*, Geneva: Droz, 1957, pp.99-102.

Bb137   Daudet, Alphonse, 'Promenades en Afrique: La mule du
         Cadi' I, *Le Monde Illustré* (27.12.1862).

Bb138   Daudet, Léon, ['EF'], *L'Action Française* (8.9.1926); repr.
         in *Ecrivains et artistes*, Paris: Edns du Capitole, 1928, vol. II,
         pp. 215-24.

Bb139   —, Refs in *Mes idées esthétiques*, Paris: A. Fayard, 1939,
         passim.

         Daudy, Philippe: see Ab24.

Bb140   Dauger, Alfred, 'Salon de 1851', *Le Pays* (23.2.1851).

         Davesnes, Armand: see Ab43.

Bb141   Dax, P., 'Chroniques', *L'Artiste* (15.8.1863; 15.9.1863;
         1.5.1866; 1.3.1877).

Bb142   Debien, G., 'Deux grands-oncles de F à Saint-Domingue', in
         Ba31, pp.75-100.

Bb143   Deffoux, Léon, 'Le Cinquantenaire de F', *Mercure de France*,
         CXC, 677 (1.9.1926), 503.

Bb144   —, 'Les Personnages de *Dominique'*, *ibid.*, CXCVI, 694
         (15.5.1927), 255-6.

Bb145   Degoumois, Léon, Refs in *L'Algérie d'Alphonse Daudet*,
         Geneva: Edns 'Sonor', S.A., 1922, *passim*.

Bb146   Delaborde, Henri, in *Mélanges sur l'art contemporain*, Paris:
         Renouard, 1866, pp.29-30, 137, 194-5.

Bb147   De Lagenevais, 'Le Salon de 1849', *RDM* (15.8.1849), 575.*

Bb148   Delancre, Pierre, '*Dominique* ou la cohérence en creux', *Revue
         des Sciences Humaines*, XXXVI, 143 (July-Sept. 1971), 373-80.

Bb149   Delay, Jean, Ref. in *La Jeunesse d'André Gide*, Paris:
         Gallimard, 1956-7, vol. II, p.288.

         Demaison, André: see Ba1.

Bb150   Denormandie, Ernest, in *Temps passé, jours présents: Notes
         de famille*, Paris: Société anonyme de publications périodiques,
         1900, pp.181-7. See also Ab2.

Denux, Roger: see Ab27.

Deschamps, Gaston: see Ba30.4.

Bb151 De Smedt, Raphaël, 'Mechelen als Inspiratiebron in de Franse Literatuur' [Gautier, Hugo, Nerval, Taine, Nisard, Baudelaire, F, C. Lemonnier], *Handelingen van de Kon, Kring voor Oudheidkunde Letteren en Kunst van Mechelen* (1967), 64-92.*

Bb152 Deville, Jacques, 'La Passion de jeunesse d'EF', in Ba15.

Bb153 Dézamy, Adrien, 'F: Chasse au faucon', [Poem inspired by F's painting on this subject], in *Les Chefs-d'œuvre d'art au Luxembourg* [coll. ed. by Eugène Montrosier], Paris: Baschet, 1881, interleaved between pp.14 & 15.

Bb154 Dorbec, Prosper, 'La Sensibilité de l'artiste dans *Dominique*', *Revue Bleue* (6.11.1920), 645-9.

Bb155 —, 'L'Héllenisme d'EF', *GBA* (Jan. 1924), 30-8.

Bb156 —, 'La Méthode de l'écrivain chez EF', *Revue d'Histoire Littéraire de la France* (July-Sept. 1924), 448-56.

Doris: see Nebout.

Bb157 Dorsenne, Jean, 'EF', *Les Nouvelles Littéraires* (2.10.1926).

Bb158 Doudan, Ximénès, in *Lettres*, Paris: Lévy, 1879, vol. IV, pp.254, 278-9.

Bb159 Drumont, Edouard, 'EF', *Galerie Contemporaine, Littéraire, Artistique*, ser. II, 58-60 (1877).

Bb160 Du Bos, Charles, in *Journal*, Paris: Edns Corrêa, 1946, vol. I [1921-3], pp.38, 132-3, 193, 197, 261; 1948, vol. II [1924-5], pp.97, 298; 1949, vol. III [1926-7], pp.133-4; 1954, vol. V [1929], p.35.

Bb161 —, in Introduction to *Feuilles tombées* by René Boylesve, Paris: Edns de la Pléiade, 1927, p.38, n.1.

Bb162 Dubufe, G., 'Art et Métier: Taine et F, critiques d'art', *RDM* (15.8.1896).

Bb163 Du Camp, Maxime, 'Le Salon de 1857', *Revue de Paris* (15.7.1857), 207-8.

Bb164 —, in *Les Beaux-Arts à l'Exposition Universelle et aux Salons de 1863, 1864, 1865, 1866 et 1867*, Paris: Renouard, 1867, pp.18-21, 87-90, 165-7, 222-5, 281.

Bb165 —, in *Souvenirs littéraires*, Paris: Hachette, 1882, vol. I, p. 350; vol. II, pp.276-84.

Bb166 Duchemin, Marcel, 'Source probable d'une page de F', *Bulletin de l'Association G. Budé*, XII (Dec. 1950), 77-8.

Bb167 Duclaud, Jacques, 'EF et la politique', *L'Action Française* (25.3.1912).

Ducros: see Montibert-Ducros.

Bb168 Dugas, L., Ref. in *Les Timides dans la littérature et l'art*, Paris: Félix Alcan, 1925, p.83.

Bb169 Duhousset, E., in *Le Cheval dans la nature et dans l'art*, Paris: Laurens, 1902, vol. II, p.136 *et seq.*

Bb170 Dumesnil, Henri, in *Le Salon de 1859*, Paris: Renouard, 1859, pp.57-9.

Bb171 Dumesnil, René, in *Le Réalisme et le Naturalisme*, Paris: del Duca de Gigord, 1955, pp.15, 105, 119-23, 125, 145, 201.

Bb172 Du Pays, A. J., 'Salon de 1864', *L'Illustration*, II (July-Oct. 1864).

Bb173 Duplessis, Georges, '*Les Maîtres d'autrefois*', *Polybiblion*, Ser. II, IV, 37.

Dupont, Léonce: see Ba30.2.

Bb174 Dupouy, Auguste, 'De F aux frères Tharaud', *Démocratie Nouvelle* (27.1.1923).

Bb175 Duproix, J.-J., 'La Personnalité d'EF', *Bibliothèque Universelle et Revue Suisse*, LV (Aug. 1909), 332-67.

Bb176 Durand-Dautan, Pierre, 'Un Maître de la critique en peinture', *Démocratie Nouvelle* (18.11.1920).

Bb177 Duranty, Edmond, in *La Nouvelle Peinture (1876)*, Paris: Librairie Floury, 1946, pp.22-4.

Bb178 Duret, Théodore, in *Les Peintres français en 1867*, Paris: Dentu, 1867, pp.50-6.

Bb179 Duvergier de Hauranne, Ernest, 'La Peinture française au Salon de 1872', *RDM* (15.6.1872), p.855.

Bb180 ——, 'Le Salon de 1874', *RDM* (1.6.1874), p.678.

Bb181 Duviard, Ferdinand, 'EF, peintre littéraire de l'Aunis', lecture broadcast from Bordeaux-Lafayette (23.4.1937).

Bb182 E, B., '*Dominique*', *Revue Contemporaine* (31.3.1863).*

Bb183 Eckford, H., 'EF', *Century Magazine*, III (1883), 829-38.

Bb184   Ernest-Charles, J., 'EF' [CR of Ba2], *La Grande Revue* (10.10.1911), 616-21.

Bb185   Evans, Arthur Robert (Jr), 'The Art of Narrative in F's *Dominique*', *Modern Language Notes*, LXXIX, 3 (May 1964), 270-6; also in Ba9, pp.22-30.

Bb186   Faggi, Adolfo, 'Nel primo centenario di EF', *Il Marzocco* (14.11.1920).

Bb187   Faguet, Emile, 'EF: l'homme. (Souvenirs intimes)', in Ba30, pp.9-10.

Bb188   —, 'La Jeunesse d'EF', *RDM* (1.4.1909), 599-614.

Bb189   Fairlie, Alison, CR of Ab23, *Modern Language Review*, LXII, 3 (July 1967), 534-5.

Bb190   Faral, Edmond, 'Deux pages de F et de Théophile Gautier', *Revue d'Histoire Littéraire de la France* (July-Sept. 1911), 672-3.

Bb191   Félix-Faure-Goyau, Lucie, 'F', *Journal de l'Université des Annales*, XII (1.6.1911), 680-96; repr. in *Journal des Demoiselles* (1.12.1911).

Bb192   Ferran, André, Refs in *L'Esthétique de Baudelaire*, Paris: Hachette, 1933, pp.31, 410, 421-2.

Bb193   Ferrucci, Franco, 'F e l'immobile felicità', *Rivista di letterature moderne e comparate*, XVII, 3 (Sept. 1964), 178-96.

Bb194   Ferte, René de la, 'Chroniques', *L'Artiste* (1.3.1868; 1.6.1868; 1.2.1869).*

Bb195   Fiorioli, E., 'Le Centenaire de *Dominique*', *Culture française* [Bari], IX (1962), 35-7.*

Bb196   Flers, Robert de, 'En marge de *Dominique*', in Ba16.

Bb197   Fosca, François, 'F', in *De Diderot à Valéry: les écrivains et les arts visuels*, Paris: Albin Michel, 1960, pp.211-31.

Foucart, Jacques: see Ab51.

Bb198   Fournel, Victor, in *Les Artistes français contemporains*, Tours: Mame, 1884, pp.379-89.

Fournier: see Alain-Fournier.

Fraigneau, André: see Ab26.

Bb199   Francotte, Henri, 'EF: *Dominique*', *Revue Générale*, XXVIII (1878), 219-36.

Bb200　Frank, Félix, *'Dominique'*, *RDM* (15.7.1863), 473.

Bb201　Gaillard de Champris, Henry, 'La Vraie Leçon de *Dominique* et le Classicisme de F', in *Anniversaires et Pèlerinages*, Quebec: *L'Action Sociale*, 1922, pp.65-89.

Bb202　Gambier, P., 'Un Ami de F: Félix Sainton', *Revue du Bas-Poitou et des Provinces de l'Ouest*, LXVII, (April 1956), 100-16. See also Ac12.

Bb203　Ganne, Gilbert, 'F, Janus de l'art: Entretien avec Erik Dahl', *Nouvelles Littéraires* (13.8.1970); repr. in *Bernanos, Giraudoux, Barrès, Claudel, Matisse, Maurras, Fromentin, La Varende, Feydeau, Loti, tels que les voient leurs héritiers*, Paris: Plon, 1972, pp.165-84.

Bb204　Garcin, Philippe, 'Le Souvenir dans *Dominique*', *NRF* (1.1.1957), 111-21.

Bb205　Gaubert, Ernest, 'EF et l'influence de *Dominique*', *Mercure de France* (1.10.1905), 321-34; repr. in *Figures françaises*, Paris: Nouvelle Librairie Nationale, 1910, pp.41-69.

Bb206　Gautier, Théophile, 'Musée royal du Louvre: Exposition de 1847', *La Presse* (9.4.1847).

Bb207　—, 'Salon de 1849' VIII, *La Presse* (7.8.1849).

Bb208　—, 'Salon de 1850-1' XVIII, *ibid.* (24.8.1851).

Bb209　—, 'Le Sahara', *L'Artiste* (22.2.1857), 161-4; (1.3.1857), 177-80; (1.11.1857), 129-30; repr. in *L'Orient*, Paris: Charpentier, 1877, vol. II, pp.333-72.

Bb210　—, 'Salon de 1859' VI, *Le Moniteur Universel* (28.5.1859).

Bb211　—, 'Salon de 1861' XII, *ibid.* (25.6.1861).

Bb212　—, 'Salon de 1863' IV, *ibid.* (20.6.1863).

Bb213　—, 'Salon de 1864', *ibid.* (16.7.1864).

Bb214　—, 'Salon de 1865' IX, *ibid.* (22.7.1865).

Bb215　—, 'Salon de 1866' V, *ibid.* (17.7.1866).

Bb216　—, 'Salon de 1868' V, *ibid.* (17.5.1868).

Bb217　—, 'Le Salon de 1869' III, *L'Illustration* (22.5.1869); repr. in *Tableaux à la plume*, Paris: Charpentier, 1880.

Bb218　Geffroy, Gustave, in *Les Musées d'Europe: La Hollande,* Paris: Nilsson, [n.d.], pp.58-9.*

Bb219　Geoffroy, Auguste, in *Etudes d'après F* [essays on the Sahara and the Sahel, inspired by F], Paris: Challamel aîné, 1882.

Bb220　Geoffroy, L. de, 'Le Salon de 1850', *RDM* (1.3.1851), 940.*

Bb221　George, André, *'Voyage en Egypte', Les Nouvelles Littéraires* (18.4.1936).

Bb222　Germond, Raoul, 'Les Ancêtres mauzéens d'EF', *Revue du Bas-Poitou et des Provinces de l'Ouest*, LXXVI, 3 & 4 (May-Aug. 1965), 179-86.

　　　　Gerson, H.: see Ab46.

Bb223　Gibbon, Monk, 'Sir Edward Marsh's translation of *Dominique* [Ab17]', Tredegar Memorial Lecture, 1952, in *Essays by Divers Hands: Transactions of the Royal Society of Literature* [Oxford Univ. Press], XXVII (1955), 1-20.

Bb224　—, CR of Ab23, *Irish Times* (15.10.1965).

Bb225　Gibson, Robert, Refs in *The Quest of Alain-Fournier*, London: Hamish Hamilton, 1953, pp.41, 121, 189, 211, 271.

Bb226　Gide, André, 'Les Dix Romans français que . . .', in *Incidences*, Paris: Gallimard, 1924, p.154.

Bb227　—, in *Divers*, Paris: Gallimard, 1931, pp.198-9.

Bb228　—, 'Nationalisme et littérature', in *Nouveaux prétextes*, Paris: Mercure de France, 1951 edn, p.69.

Bb229　—, Refs in *Journal*, Paris: Bibl. de la Pléiade, 1951 [1889-1939], pp.38, 901; 1954 [1939-49], p.298.

Bb230　—, Ref. in *Correspondance d'André Gide et de Paul Valéry, 1890-1942*, Paris: Gallimard, 1955, p.65.

Bb231　—, Refs in *Correspondance André Gide – Arnold Bennett, (1911-1931)*, Introduction and notes by Linette F. Brugmans, Geneva: Droz; Paris: Minard, 1964, pp.22, 65 & n.2.

Bb232　—, Ref., in a letter to Robert de Traz, quoted by Jean-Pierre Meylan in *'La Revue de Genève: Miroir des lettres européennes, 1920-30*, Geneva: Droz, 1969, pp.473-4.*

Bb233　—, Ref. in *Correspondance Rainer Maria Rilke – André Gide, 1906-1926*, ed. R. Lang, Paris: Corrêa, 1952, p.52.*

Bb234　Gigoux, Jean, in *Causeries sur les artistes de mon temps*, Paris: Calmann-Lévy, 1885, pp.268-70.

Bb235　Gille, Philippe, in *La Bataille littéraire. (1875-1878)*, Paris: Victor-Havard, 1889, Ser. I, pp.310-2.

Bb236 Gillet, Louis, 'EF et *Dominique*, d'après des documents inédits', *Revue de Paris* (1.8.1905), 526-58.

Bb237 —, 'Les Peintures d'EF', in Ba30, pp.53-61.

Bb238 —, 'A la *Royal Academy*: l'exposition d'art hollandais', *RDM* (15.2.1929), 931-46.

Bb239 —, 'F et les peintres de l'Algérie', *Revue Hebdomadaire* (23.2.1929), 387-409.

Bb240 Girard, Alain, Refs in *Le Journal intime*, Paris: Presses Universitaires de France, 1963, Bibl. de Philosophie Contemporaine, pp.30, 31, 34.

Bb241 Giraud, Victor, 'EF', *RDM* (May-June 1939); repr. in Ba11.

Bb242 —, 'EF', *Les Nouvelles Littéraires* (17.6.1939).

Bb243 Giraudeau, Fernand, '*Une Année dans le Sahel: Journal d'un absent*', *Revue Contemporaine* (15.6.1859), 567-9.

Bb244 Girrebeuk, Lucile (maiden name and pseudonym of Mme Gautronneau), 'F fut-il un peintre qui a écrit ou un écrivain qui a peint? ', lecture given to the Académie des Belles-Lettres, Sciences et Arts de La Rochelle (20.11.1963).

Gogh, Vincent van: see Bb531.

Bb245 Golliet, Pierre, 'En marge de l'idée de religion séculière: la religion de l'art (Documents)', in *Science et conscience de la société: Mélanges en l'honneur de Raymond Aron*, Paris: Calmann-Lévy, 1971, vol. I, pp.579-90.

Bb246 —, 'Rubens vu par F', lecture given to the Institut français de Budapest (8.6.1969).

Bb247 Goncourt, Edmond & Jules de, in *Journal*, Paris: Flammarion-Fasquelle, 1956, vol. II, pp.89, 217-8; vol. IV, p.54: vol. V, pp.147-9, 189, 191-2, 216, 220, 226; vol. VI, pp.129, 224, 240.

Bb248 Gonnard, Philippe, 'La Leçon de F', *Revue Bleue*, X (5.3.1910), 303-7; (12.3.1910), 334-41.

Bb249 Gonse, Louis [see also Ab1, 34, 35, 36; Ba30.4], 'Salon de 1874' II, *GBA*, X (1.7.1874), 48-9.

Bb250 —, 'EF', *La Chronique des Arts et de la Curiosité* (9.9.1876), 257.

Bb251 —, 'EF, peintre et écrivain', *GBA*, XLII (1878), 401-14; XLIII (1878), 84-91; XLIV (1879), 240-54; XLVI (1879), 281-97; XLVII (1879), 50-70, 464-80; XLVIII (1879), 139-50, 216-28, 319-33, 404-19; repr. in Ba12.

Bb252 Gougenheim, G., 'La Présentation du discours direct dans *La Princesse de Clèves* et dans *Dominique*', *Le Français Moderne*, VI, 4 (Oct. 1938), 305-20.

Bb253 Goyau, Georges, 'F et son roman *Dominique*', *Intermédiaire des Chercheurs*, LXXXII (20-30. 10. 1920), 208.

Bb254 Grandegor, J., 'Le Salon de 1868', *GBA*, XXIV (1.6.1868), 517.

Bb255 Green, F. C., in *French Novelists from the Revolution to Proust*, London: Dent, 1931, pp.268-71.

Bb256 Grenier, Edouard, ['EF'], *Revue Bleue*, LII (12.8.1893); repr. in *Souvenirs littéraires*, Paris: Lemerre, 1894, pp.326-29.

Bb257 Greshoff, C. J., 'F's *Dominique*', *Essays in Criticism*, XI, 2 (April 1961), 164-89; repr. in *Seven Studies in the French Novel, from Mme de La Fayette to Robbe-Grillet*, Cape Town: A. A. Balkema, 1964, pp.53-70.

Bb258 Grimsley, Ronald, 'Romanticism in *Dominique*', *French Studies*, XII, 1 (Jan. 1958), 44-57.

Bb259 —, CR of Ab23, *French Studies*, XX, 4 (Oct. 1966), 419-20.

Bb260 —, CR of Ab25, *French Studies*, XXII, 2 (April 1968), 173-4.

Bb261 Grisay, A., 'Le Contrat d'édition et l'originale de *Dominique*', *Le Livre et l'Estampe*, 61-2 (1970), 66-70.

Bb262 Guillemin, Henri, 'F: *Dominique*', in *A vrai dire*, Paris: Gallimard, 1956, pp.139-47.

Bb263 Gutwirth, Marcel, CR of Ba9, *French Review*, XXXIX, 1 (Oct. 1965), 175.*

Bb264 Halévy, Daniel, 'Sur une lettre de F', *Journal des Débats* (14.2.1920).

Bb265 —, in *Pays parisiens*, Paris: Edns Emile-Paul, 1929, pp.59-60.

Bb266 Haloche, Maurice, 'EF', *Le Thyrse: Revue d'Art et de Littérature* (10.10.1926), 373-5.

Bb267 Hapgood, Norman, 'EF', *Contemporary Review*, LXXVII (Feb. 1900), 277-83.

Bb268 Hautecœur, Louis, Refs in *Littérature et peinture en France, du XVIIe au XXe siècle*, Paris: Armand Colin, [1942] 2nd edn 1963, pp.100, 117, 124, 170, 187.

Bb269 Henriot, Emile [see also Ab13], 'F en Egypte', *Le Temps* (5.11.1935); repr. in *Courrier littéraire XIXe siècle: Réalistes et naturalistes*, Paris: Albin Michel, 1954, pp.140-53.

Bb270 —, 'Le Rêve et la réalité dans *Dominique*', *Le Temps* (12.5.1936).

Bb271 —, 'F et *Dominique*', *RDM* (1.10.1936), 572-95.

Hoog, Armand: see Ab15, Ab22.

Bb272 Hourticq, Louis, 'F peintre et critique', in Ba18, pp.30-4.

Bb273 Houssaye, Henry, 'EF: l'exposition de son œuvre à l'Ecole des Beaux-Arts', *RDM* (15.4.1877), 882-95.

Howald, Ernst: see Ab30.

Bb274 Hubert, Renée Riese, 'F's *Dominique*: the confession of a man who judges himself', *PMLA*, LXXXII, 7 (Dec.1967), 634-9.

Bb275 Huyghe, René, Refs in *Dialogue avec le visible*, Paris: Flammarion, 1955, pp.12, 377.

Bb276 Huysmans, J.-K., in *L'Art moderne*, Paris: Charpentier, 1883, pp.31-3.

Bb277 Hytier, Jean, in *Les Romans de l'individu*, Paris: Les Arts et le Livre, 1928, pp.135-143.

Bb278 Ideville, Henry d', 'Le Poète de l'Algérie: *Une Année dans le Sahel* par EF', *Journal de Paris* (3.8.1874).

Bb279 Ignotus [pseudonym of Félix Platel], ['EF'], *Le Figaro* (8.9.1876); repr. in *Portraits*, Paris: Cochet, 1878, pp.78-84.

Bb280 Jaloux, Edmond, 'Hommage à *Dominique*', *Le Gaulois* (29.12.1913); repr. in *De Pascal à Barrès*, Paris: Plon, 1927, pp.93-103.

Bb281 Jammes, Francis, Ref. in *Correspondance avec André Gide (1893-1938)*, Paris: Gallimard, 1948, p.186.

Bb282 Jamot, Paul, 'Pourquoi F a-t-il voulu être peintre?', *Revue Universelle*, XXXII (1.1.1928), 113-20.

Bb283 Janssens, René, 'Les Maîtres de la critique d'art', *Académie royale de Belgique, Classe des Beaux-Arts: Mémoires*, Ser. II, IV (1935), 66-8.

Bb284 Japon, Jacques, 'Le Village de Saint-Maurice ou un souvenir du Romantisme', *Courrier du Sud-Ouest* (19.11.1948).

Bb285 Jouin, Henry, in *Maîtres contemporains*, Paris: Perrin, 1887, pp. 1-81.

Bb286   Jourda, Pierre, 'L'Exotisme dans la littérature française depuis Chateaubriand', *Revue des Cours et Conférences*, IV (28.2.1939), 544-9; V (15.3.1939), 651-2.

Bb287   Jullian, Philippe, Ref. in *Robert de Montesquiou: A fin-de-siècle prince*, London: Secker & Warburg, 1967 [Eng. tr., by John Haylock and Francis King, of *Un prince 1900: Robert de Montesquiou*, Paris: Librairie Académique Perrin, 1965], p.117.

Bb288   ——, 'Charles Haas', *GBA*, LXXVII (April 1971), p.250.

Bb289   Kereyen, ['EF'], *Intermédiaire des Chercheurs*, LXXXII (20-30.12.1920), 415-7.

Bb290   Knapp, Lothar, '*Roman personnel* und romantische *sensibilité*: Constant, Musset, F', *Zeitschrift für französische Sprache und Literatur*, LXXXI (1971), 98-135.*

Bb291   Küchler, W., 'EF', *Süddeutsche Monatshefte* (Dec. 1906), 589-604.

Bb292   Lacretelle, Jacques de, Ref. quoted by Pierre Varillon and Henri Rambaud in *Enquête sur les maîtres de la jeune littérature*, Paris: Bloud et Gay, 1923, pp.85-6.

Bb293   Lafenestre, Georges, in *Artistes et amateurs*, Paris: Société d'édn artistique, [n.d.], pp.324-5.

Bb294   Lafont, R., CR of Ba9, *Revue des Langues Romanes*, LXXVII (1966), 258-9.*

Bb295   Lagrange, Léon, 'Le Salon de 1861' [IV], *GBA*, XI (1.7.1861).

Bb296   ——, 'Le Salon de 1864' [II] *GBA*, XVII (1.7.1864).

Bb297   Lalou, René, 'De Descartes à Proust: L'Idée de l'homme dans le roman psychologique français', in *Défense de l'homme (intelligence et sensualité)*, Paris: Edns du Sagittaire, Kra, 1926, pp.212-4.

Bb298   Lanson, Gustave, Ref. in *L'Art de la prose*, Paris: Librairie des Annales, 1909, p.263.

Bb299   Lapauze, Henry, 'EF', *Le Gaulois* (1.10.1905); repr. in *La Renaissance Politique, Littéraire, Artistique* (30.10.1920).

Bb300   Lapeyre, André, 'EF', in Ba31, pp.67-74.

Bb301   Larthomas, P., CR of Ba9, *Le Français Moderne*, XXXV (1967), 148-9.*

Bb302   La Salle, B. de, 'En marge du centenaire de *Dominique*: mourir d'amour? ', *Les Nouvelles Littéraires* (3.1.1963), 3.*

Bb303   Lasserre, Pierre, 'EF', *L'Action Française* (16.2.1909); repr. in *Portraits et Discussions*, Paris: Mercure de France, 1914, pp.62-72.

Bb304   Lasteyrie, F. de, ['EF'], *Le Siècle* (27.7.1862).*

Bb305   Latiolais, F. M., 'Not quite a Masterpiece: F's *Dominique* Reconsidered', *Mosaic*, IV, 1 (Fall 1970) [Winnipeg, Univ. of Manitoba Press], 35-48.

Bb306   Lebel, Roland, in *Histoire de la littérature coloniale en France*, Paris: Larose, 1931, pp.60-1, 93-4.

Bb307   Le Breton, André, 'F en Algérie', *Revue des Cours et Conférences* (30.12.1928), 97-111.

Bb308   Lechalas, G., 'Les Années d'apprentissage d'EF', *L'Année Philosophique* (1911), 9-38.

Bb309   —, 'Les Années de maturité d'EF', *ibid.* (1913), 61-89.

Bb310   Le Hir, Yves, 'Un aspect de la sensibilité de F dans *Dominique*', *Mercure de France* (Oct. 1957), 286-92.

Bb311   Leleu, Michèle, Refs in *Les Journaux intimes*, Paris: Presses Universitaires de France, 1952, pp.9, 12.

Bb312   Lerat, A., 'Le Centenaire de *Dominique*' [account of Bb241], *Le Sud-Ouest* (25.11.1963).

Bb313   Leroi, Paul, '*Vade Mecum* du Salon de 1876', *L'Art*, V (1876), p.152.

Bb314   Levallois, Jules, 'Romans nouveaux et jeunes romanciers', *L'Opinion Nationale* (22.3.1863).

Bb315   Lévêque, Jean-Jacques, 'EF à La Rochelle: un maître d'autrefois', *Les Nouvelles Littéraires* (13.8.1970).

Bb316   Lhote, André, 'Extraits d'*Une Année dans le Sahel*, avec notice', in *De la palette à l'écritoire*, Paris: Edns Corrêa, 1946, pp.207-23. See also Ab45.

Bb317   Lionnet, Jean, 'Flaubert et F: lettres de jeunesse', *Revue Hebdomadaire* (15.5.1909), 398-401.

Bb318   Lugli, Vittorio, Ref. in *Bovary italiane e altri saggi*, Caltanissetta-Rome: S. Sciascia Editore, 1959, Aretusa: Collezione di letteratura, No. 10.*

Bb319 MacCarthy, Henri, 'Notice biographique sur Oscar MacCarthy, géographe', *Revue Africaine*, II (1913), p.197.

Bb320 Magowan, Robin, 'F and Jewett: Pastoral Narrative in the Nineteenth Century', *Comparative Literature*, XVI (Fall 1964), 331-7.

Bb321 Maire, Gilbert, Refs in *Les Instants privilégiés*, Paris: Edns Montaigne, 1962, pp.144, 145-6, 155, 156-67, 168, 169, 181, 194, 200, 224, 231, 414.

Bb322 Mantz, Paul, 'Le Salon de 1859', *GBA* (1.6.1859).

Bb323 —, 'Le Salon de 1863', *GBA* (1.6.1863), 496-8.

Bb324 —, 'Le Salon de 1865', *GBA* (1.6.1865), 520.

Bb325 —, 'Le Salon de 1867', *GBA* (1.6.1867), 530.

Bb326 —, 'Le Salon de 1872', *GBA* (1.7.1872), 47.

Bb327 Marchou, Gaston, '*Dominique*, chef-d'œuvre de l'impossible, a cent ans', *Revue de Paris*, LXX (Sept. 1963), 74-81.

Bb328 Martino, Pierre, 'Les Descriptions de F', *Revue Africaine* (1910), 343-92.

Bb329 —, 'F: essai de bibliographie critique', *ibid.* (1914),153-82.

Bb330 —, 'Le Centenaire de F', *ibid.* (1920), 140-57.

Bb331 —, 'La Littérature algérienne', in *Histoire et Historiens de l'Algérie*, Paris: Félix Alcan, 1931, pp.338-40.

Bb332 Marye, Edouard, '*Dominique*', *Les Nouvelles Littéraires* (25.2.1933).

Bb333 Masqueray, Emile, in *Souvenirs et visions d'Afrique*, Paris: E. Dentu, 1894, pp.183-99.

Bb334 Massa, Alexandre-Philippe, Marquis de, 'La Cour des Tuileries', *Revue Hebdomadaire* (22.1.1910), 444-70.

Bb335 Massis, Henri, '*Dominique* ou la confession inutile', *Revue Universelle* (15.11.1920); repr. in *Jugements*, Paris: Plon, 1924, pp.283-92.

Bb336 —, 'Le Cas de *Dominique*: le faux roman, c'est l'autobiographie', *Comœdia* (17.11.1926).

Bb337 Massot, Pierre de, 'De la plume au pinceau: F', *Les Nouvelles Littéraires* (24.7.1937).

Bb338 Matheron, Laurent, in *Exposition de la Société des Amis des Arts, 1852: revue critique*, Bordeaux: chez les principaux libraires, 1852, p.29.

Bb339 —, in *Exposition de la Société des Amis des Arts, 1853: revue critique*, Bordeaux: chez les principaux libraires, 1853, pp.39-40.

Bb340 Mathieu, Pierre-Louis, 'Documents inédits sur la jeunesse de Gustave Moreau (1826-1860)' [based on lecture, under same title, given, in Paris, to the Société d'Histoire de l'Art français (6.11.1971)], *Bulletin de la Société d'Histoire de l'Art français* [année 1971] (1972), 270-7.

Bb341 Mauriac, Claude, 'EF: *Dominique*', in *De la littérature à l'alittérature*, Paris: Grasset, 1969, pp.333-42.

Bb342 Mauriac, François, Ref. in *Mémoires intérieurs*, Paris: Flammarion, 1959, p.148.

Bb343 —, 'Les Bâtons rompus de la fièvre', *Le Figaro Littéraire* (30.1.1960).

Bb344 Maury, Lucien, 'De F à Loti', *Revue Bleue* (27.2.1909), 279-82.

Bb345 Maynial, Edouard, 'EF, son œuvre d'écrivain', *Revue Générale,* LXXIX (March 1904), 387-403.

Bb346 Mazade, Charles de, 'Chronique de la quinzaine', *RDM* (1.9.1857), 217.

Bb347 McLaren, J. C., CR of Ba9, *L'Esprit Créateur*, VI (1966), 126-7.*

Bb348 Mein, Margaret, 'F, a Precursor of Proust', *Forum for Modern Language Studies*, VII, 3 (July 1971), 221-36.

Bb349 Mellerio, André, 'Trois peintres écrivains: Delacroix, F, Odilon Redon', *La Nouvelle Revue* (15.4.1923), 303-14.

Menanteau, Pierre: see Ab21.

Bb350 Ménard, René, 'Collection Laurent Richard' [2] , *GBA* (1.4.1873), 326-7.*

Bb351 Merlant, Joachim [see also Ba30.4] , in *Le Roman personnel, de Rousseau à F,* Paris: Hachette, 1905, pp.412-6.

Bb352 —, in *Senancour: sa vie, son œuvre, son influence*, Paris: Fischbacher, 1907, pp.308-9.

Mérys, Jacques-André: pseudonym of Pierre Blanchon (q.v.).

Bb353 Michel, Emile, in *Les Maîtres du paysage*, Paris: Hachette, 1906, pp.496-9 & *passim.*

Bb354 Moisy, Pierre [see also Ab52, Ac13] , 'F devant les Maîtres des anciens Pays-Bas', lecture given to the Académie des Belles - Lettres de La Rochelle (23.1.1969).

Bb355   —, 'F, écrivain-peintre', in Ba7, pp.iv-xiv; repr. in Ba31, pp.9-18.

Bb356   Mombello, G., CR of Bb556, *Studi Francesi* (1965), 175.

Bb357   —, CR of Bb193, *Studi Francesi* (1966), 172.

Bb358   —, CR of Bb454, *Studi Francesi* (1966), 172.

Bb359   —, CR of Ba9, *Studi Francesi* (1966), 377-8.

Bb360   —, CR of Ab38, *Studi Francesi* (1966), 378.

Bb361   —, CR of Ab25, *Studi Francesi* (1969), 169.

Bb362   Mondon, René, 'F à l'Académie de La Rochelle', in Ba31, pp.37-42.

         Mondor, Henri: see Ab19.

Bb363   Monge, Jacques, 'Un Précurseur de Proust: F et la mémoire affective', *Revue d'Histoire Littéraire de la France* (Oct. - Dec. 1961), 564-88.

Bb364   —, CR of Ba9, *Revue d'Histoire Littéraire de la France* (Oct.-Dec. 1966), 737.

Bb365   Monglond, André, in *Le Journal intime d'Oberman*, Paris & Grenoble: Arthaud, 1947, pp.43-4.

Bb366   Montégut, Emile, 'De la littérature des voyages: un artiste français en Afrique', *RDM* (15.6.1860), 889-905.

Bb367   —, 'EF, écrivain', *RDM*, XXIV (1877), 674-91; repr. in *Nos morts contemporains*, Paris: Hachette, 1884, Ser. II, pp.77-111.

Bb368   Montibert-Ducros, Carmen, 'EF, touche-à-tout de génie', *Jardin des Arts*, 187 (June 1970), 48-55.

Bb369   —, 'Introduction à l'œuvre picturale de F', in Ba7, pp.xxi-xxxiv; repr. in Ba31, pp.25-36.

Bb370   Montifaud, Marc de, 'Le Salon de 1865', *L'Artiste* (1.6.1865), 244.

Bb371   Morcos, Fouad, 'F et la double vision picturale et littéraire de l'Orient', *Revue de l'Université Laurentienne* [Sudbury, Ontario] II, 2 (Nov. 1969), 109-14; III, 1 (June 1970), 87-94.*

Bb372   Moreau, Pierre, 'De quelques paysages introspectifs', in *Formen der Selbstdarstellung: Analekten zu einer Geschichte des Literarischen Selbsportraits*, Festgabe für Fritz Neubert, Berlin: Duncker & Humblot, 1956, pp.281, 283, 285.

Bb373   —, in *Amours romantiques*, Paris: Hachette, 1963, Coll. 'L'Amour et l'Histoire', pp.130, 146-50.

Bb374 —, Ref. in *Ames et thèmes romantiques*, Paris: Corti, 1965, p.19.

Bb375 —, 'De la *Philosophie de l'art* aux *Maîtres d'autrefois*, ou l'école des sensations', in *De Jean Lemaire de Belges à Jean Giraudoux: Mélanges d'histoire et de critique littéraire offerts à Pierre Jourda*, Paris: Nizet, 1970, pp.359-74.

Bb376 Moreau-Nelaton, Etienne, in *Bonvin raconté par lui-même*, Paris: Laurens, 1927, pp.92, 93, 94.

Bb377 Morgan, Charles, 'An Old Novel Re-born', *The Hibbert Journal* (April 1949); repr. in *The Writer and his World: Lectures and Essays*, London: Macmillan, 1960, pp.207-19.

Bb378 Morland, Jacques, 'F d'après sa correspondance', *L'Opinion* (27.4.1912).

Bb379 Moulin, Charles, 'EF', *La Tribune de l'Aunis* (6.7.1970).

Mraz, Bohumir: see Ab50.

Muller, Henry: see Ab20.

Bb380 N., 'A propos d'EF', *L'Afrique Nouvelle* (10.10.1909).

Bb381 Navarre, Charles, 'EF', *Monde et Voyage* (1.2.1933). See also Ab12.

Bb382 Nebout, Pierre [unfinished article published by André Doris], 'Les romans de ceux qui ne sont pas du métier', *Démocratie Nouvelle* (19.12.1920).

Bb383 Nerlich, M., CR of Ba9, *Romanische Forschungen*, LXXVII (1966), 454-6.*

Neumann, Jaromir: see Ab50.

Bb384 Nicolle, Henri, 'Un Eté dans le Sahara', *Le Pays* (14.5.1857).

Bb385 Nugent, Robert, CR of Ba9, *Modern Language Journal*, XLIX, 7 (Nov. 1965), 447-8.*

Bb386 O'Brien, Justin, Refs in *The Novel of Adolescence in France*, New York: Columbia Univ. Press, 1937, pp.151-2, 172-3.

Bb387 Ollivier, A., 'EF', *Bulletin Religieux du Diocèse de La Rochelle* (14.2.1903; 11.4.1903).

Bb388 Orfremont, 'F et son roman *Dominique*', *Intermédiaire des Chercheurs*, LXXXII (20-30.11.1920), p.306.

Bb389   Orlando, Francesco, in *Infanzia, memoria e storia da Rousseau ai romantici*, Padua: Liviana Editrice, 1966.*

Bb390   Pailhès, Georges, 'Le Modèle de *Dominique*', *Revue Bleue* (13.3.1909), 330-3; (20.3.1909), 358-62.

Bb391   —, 'Lettre au directeur de la *Revue bleue*', *ibid.* (26.6.1909), 828.

Bb392   Pailleron, Edouard, in *Discours de réception à l'Académie française: 17 janvier 1884*, Paris: Calmann-Lévy, 1884.*

Bb393   Pailleron, Marie-Louise, 'Deux tombes', *Le Figaro* (10.11.1921).

Bb394   Paladilhe, Jean, Refs in *Gustave Moreau* [followed by 'Gustave Moreau au regard changeant des générations', by José Pierre], Paris: Fernand Hazan, 1971, pp.13-4, 19, 22-3, 31, 37-8, 40.

Bb395   Papenbrock, J., CR of Ba9, *Beiträge zur romanischen Philologie*, VI, 11 (1967), 197-9.*

Bb396   Paret, Pierre, 'Redécouvrir EF: Là Rochelle célèbre son 150e anniversaire', *Le Sud-Ouest* (27.6.1970).

Bb397   Parvillez, Alphonse de, '*Voyage en Egypte*', *Etudes* (5.2.1936).

Bb398   Peyre, Henri, Refs in *Literature and Sincerity* [Yale Romanic Studies, Ser. II, 9], New Haven & London: Yale Univ. Press; Paris: Presses Universitaires de France, 1963, pp.172, 196-8, 200, 201.

Bb399   —, in *Qu'est-ce que le Romantisme?*, Paris: Presses Universitaires de France, 1971, Coll. Littérature Modernes, pp.244-6 & *passim*.

Bb400   Peyre, Roger, 'F', *Revue Dilecta* (1.12.1907), 113-9.

        Peyre de Betouzet, H.: see Ab40.

Bb401   Phillimore, J. S., 'EF', *Dublin Review*, CXLIV (1909), 88-110.

Bb402   Picard, Gaston [see also Ba1], 'EF vu par Charles Blanc, son rival heureux à l'Académie', in Ba16.

Bb403   —, 'Un Cinquantenaire: l'écrivain chez EF', *La Renaissance Politique, Littéraire, Artistique* (28.8.1926).

Bb404   —, 'Le Souvenir dans *Dominique* (avec une lettre inédite d'EF)', *Le Figaro* (14.12.1929). See also Ac11.

Bb405   —, 'Le Deuxième Centenaire de l'Académie de La Rochelle', *Le Figaro* (21.12.1932).

Bb406   Pichois, Claude,   Ref. in *L'Image de Jean-Paul Richter dans les lettres françaises*, Paris: Corti, 1963, p.97.

Bb407   Pierquin, Hubert,   'EF', *L'Art et les Artistes*, 106 (April 1930), 217-21.

Bb408   Pilon, Edmond,   'A propos du centenaire de F: le pèlerinage de *Dominique*', *RDM*, LIX (1920), 839-62; repr. in *Figures françaises et littéraires*, Paris: La Renaissance du livre, [1921], pp.152-84.

Bb409   —,   '*Dominique*, ou la jeunesse de F', *Revue Bleue* (19.5.1928), 291-6.

Bb410   —,   'F peintre et littérateur',   *A.B.C. artistique et littéraire* (Dec. 1930), 384-7.

Bb411   Pinot, Virgile,   'F et *Dominique*', *Revue de Hongrie* (15.5.1911), 539-56.

Bb412   Pittaluga, Mary,   'EF e le origini della moderna critica d'arte', *L'Arte*, XXI (Oct. 1918), 145-89. See also Ab42.

Bb413   Place, Joseph,   'La Faute de *Dominique*', *Bulletin du Bibliophile*, 2 (1950), 78-82. See also Ab9.

        Platel, Félix: see Ignotus.

Bb414   Pons, Roger,   '*Dominique* de F', *L'Anneau d'Or* (Nov. - Dec. 1958).

Bb415   Pouilliart, R.,   CR of Ab25,   *Les Lettres Romanes*, XXIV, 3 (1970), 306-7.

Bb416   Premonville, G. de,   'EF (1820-1876)', *Courrier Français du Sud-Ouest* (21.3.1959; 4.4.1959).

Bb417   Prévost, Marcel,   'Le Roman français au XIXe siècle', *Revue Bleue*, XIII (14.4.1900), 449-56.

Bb418   Prinet, Gaston,   'F et son roman *Dominique*', *Intermédiaire des Chercheurs*, LXXXIX (Sept. 1926), 705.

Bb419   —,   'F et son roman *Dominique*', *ibid.*, XC (10.2.1927), 129.

Bb420   —,   'F et son roman *Dominique*', *ibid.*, XCIII (August 1930), 653-4.

Bb421   Proust, Marcel,   Ref. in Preface and notes accompanying his translation of John Ruskins's *Sesame and Lilies*, presented as *Sésame et les lys*, Paris: Mercure de France, 1906, p.90, n.1.

Bb422   —,   Ref. in Preface to Bb63, p.xxi.

Bb423   —,   Ref. in *Pastiches et mélanges*, Paris: Gallimard, 1919, p.265.

Bb424   —, Refs in *Correspondance générale*, ed. Robert Proust & Paul Brach, Paris: Plon, 1932, vol. III, pp.106, 123, 125.

Bb425   —, Refs in *A un ami: correspondance inédite, 1903-1922*, Preface by Georges de Lauris, Paris: Amiot-Dumont, 1948, pp.53, 129.

Bb426   —, Ref. in *Correspondance avec sa mère, 1887-1905*, ed. Philippe Kolb, Paris: Plon, 1953, p.202.

Bb427   —, Refs in *A la recherche du temps perdu*, ed. Pierre Clarac & André Ferré, Paris: Gallimard, 1954, Bibl. de la Pléiade, vol. II, p.327; vol. III, pp.709, 809.

Bb428   —, Ref. in *Lettres à Reynaldo Hahn*, ed. Philippe Kolb, Paris; Gallimard, 1956, p.191.

Bb429   Read, Herbert, 'The Art of Art Criticism', in *The Tenth Muse: Essays in Criticism*, London: Routledge & Kegan Paul, 1957, pp.22-5. Text of a lecture broadcast on the B.B.C. Third Programme (April 1954).

Bb430   Redon, Odilon, 'Salon de 1868', *La Gironde* (1.7.1868).

Bb431   —, in *A soi-même: Journal (1867-1915)*, Introduction by Jacques Morland, Paris: Floury, 1922, pp.137-8.

Bb432   Régis, Louis, '*Une Année dans le Sahel, Un Eté dans le Sahara*', *Le Moniteur Universel* (19.2.1875; 22.2.1875).

Bb433   Renan, Ary, Refs in *Gustave Moreau (1826-1898)*, Paris: Edns de la *GBA*, 1900, pp.13, 130, 132-3.

Bb434   Renauld, Jeanne-Frédérique, 'Gabriele d'Annunzio tributaire d'EF', *Revue de Littérature Comparée* (April - June 1953), 204-11.

Bb435   Revon, Maxime, 'A propos d'un centenaire: l'expérience de F', *Les Marges*, XIX, 77 (15.11.1920), 227-30. See also Ab6, Ab14, Ab53.

Bb436   Reynaud, Camille, 'La Genèse de *Dominique*', *Annales de l'Université de Grenoble* (1936); repr. in Ba32.

Bb437   Rhodes, Samuel A., 'Sources of EF's *Dominique*', *PMLA*, XLV (Sept. 1930), 939-49.

Bb438   Richard, Jean-Pierre, 'Paysages de F', in *Littérature et sensation*, Paris: Edns du Seuil, 1954, pp.221-62.

Bb439   Richardson, Joanna, Refs in *Princess Mathilde*, London: Weidenfeld & Nicolson, 1969, pp.140-1, 235.

Bb440   Rigaud, Hippolyte, ['EF'], *Journal des Débats* (May 1855).*

Bb441   Rivière, Jacques & Alain-Fournier, Refs in *Correspondance*, Paris: Gallimard, 1926, vol. I [1905-1906], p.170; vol. IV [1908-1914], p.127. See also Bb5.

Bb442   Robaut, Alfred, Refs in *L'Œuvre de Corot*, Paris: Léonce Laget, 1965, vol. I, pp.220, 224, 240, 304, 336.

Bb443   Romero, Jorge, 'EF pintor y literato rochelés', *El Comercio* [Lima] (2.8.1931).

Bb444   Romus, André, 'F critique d'art', *Marche romane,* XII, 1 (Jan. - March 1962), 19-24.

Bb445   Rosenthal, Léon, *'Le Salon de 1845* d'EF', *La Revue de l'Art ancien et moderne*, XXVIII (July - Dec. 1910), 367-80.

Bb446   —, Refs in *Du Romantisme au réalisme: essai sur l'évolution de la peinture en France de 1830 à 1848*, Paris: Laurens, 1914, *passim*.

        Rotzler, Willy: see Ab44.

Bb447   Rouch, J., in *Orages et tempêtes dans la littérature*, Paris: Société d'édns géographiques, maritimes et coloniales, 1929, pp.153-89.

Bb448   Rousseau, Jean, 'EF', *L'Art*, VIII (1877), 11-16, 25-32.

Bb449   S., 'EF', *Journal des Débats* (8.4.1909; 26.4.1909).

Bb450   Sabord, Noël, 'Le Pays d'Ouest, Aunis, Saintonge, Angoumois, Poitou', *Les Nouvelles Littéraires* (6.10.1923).

Bb451   Sackville-West, Edward, 'Books in General', *The New Statesman and Nation*, XXI, 533 (10.5.1941), 486, 488.

Bb452   —, 'Perfect Portrait of a Gentleman', *The Listener*, XXXVIII, 980 (6.11.1947), 824-5.

Bb453   —, 'An Elegiac Novel', in *Inclinations*, London: Secker & Warburg, 1949, pp.182-8.

Bb454   Sagnes, Guy [see also Ab28], 'F et le premier *Dominique*', *Bulletin de la Société toulousaine d'études classiques* (Dec.1962); repr. in *Annales publiées par la Faculté des Lettres et Sciences humaines de Toulouse*, Littératures, XI (1964), 87-106.

Bb455   —, 'Baudelaire, Armand du Mesnil et la pétition de 1866: lettres inédites', *Revue d'Histoire Littéraire de la France* (April - June 1967), 296-309.

Bb456 ——, CR of Ab25, *ibid.* (Sept. - Oct. 1968), 860-1.

Bb457 ——, in *L'Ennui dans la littérature française de Flaubert à Laforgue (1848-1884)*, Paris: Armand Colin, 1969, pp.103-5, 130-4 & *passim*.

Bb458 ——, 'F et le silence', in Ba31, pp.43-64. Text of a lecture given to the Académie de La Rochelle (10.6.1970).

Saint-Affrique, Olga de: see Ba7.

Bb459 Sainte-Beuve, Charles-Augustin, *'Un Eté dans le Sahara, Une Année dans le Sahel'*, *Le Constitutionnel* (1.2.1864); repr. in *Nouveaux Lundis*, Paris: Lévy, 1867, pp.102-26.

Bb460 ——, *'Dominique'*, *Le Constitutionnel* (8.2.1864); repr. in *Nouveaux Lundis*, Paris: Lévy, 1867, pp.127-48.

Bb461 ——, Refs in *Correspondance générale de Sainte-Beuve*, ed. Jean Bonnerot, Paris: Aux Edns Edouard Privat, à la Librairie Marcel Didier, 1961, vol. XI [1858-1860], pp.258-9; vol. XIII [1863-1864], pp.410, 423.

Bb462 Saint-Girons, C., 'F peintre et paysagiste dans *Dominique*', *Les Cahiers de l'Ouest*, 13 (Sept. 1956), 52-5.

Bb463 Saint-Victor, Paul de, 'Salon de 1857', *La Presse* (30.8.1857).

Bb464 ——, 'Salon de 1859', *ibid.* (25.6.1859).

Bb465 ——, 'Salon de 1861', XIII, *ibid.* (28.7.1861).

Bb466 Salardaine, André, 'En manière de préface', in Ba31, pp.5-8. Text of address given on the occasion of the opening of the F Exhibitions in La Rochelle (30.5.1970). See also Ba7.

Bb467 Salaün, Jean, 'De tout . . . un peu: pour mieux connaître la Cathédrale'; *L'Appel du Vieux Clocher*, Bulletin Paroissial de la Cathédrale St Louis de La Rochelle, CCXI, 4 (April 1952).

Bb468 Sand, George [see also Ac3], *'Un Eté dans le Sahara'*, *La Presse* (8.5.1857); repr. in *Autour de la table*, Paris: Dentu, [n.d.], pp.245-52.

Bb469 ——, *'Une Année dans le Sahel'*, *La Presse* (10.3.1859); repr. in *Autour de la table*, Paris: Dentu, [n.d.], pp.253-63.

Sandoz, Marc: see Ba8.

Bb470 Sandström, Sven, Refs in *Le Monde imaginaire d'Odilon Redon*, [French tr. by Denise Naert], Lund: Cwk Gleerup, 1955, pp.19, 93, 191.

Bb471 Sarrazin, Gabriel, 'Les Personnages de second plan dans le *Dominique* de F', *Corymbe* (July - Aug. 1934), 8-11.

Bb472 Sartre, Jean-Paul, Ref. in 'Qu'est-ce que la littérature?' in *Situations*, II, Paris: Gallimard, 1948, p.180.

Bb473 ——, Ref. in *L'Idiot de la famille*, Paris: Gallimard, 1971, vol. I, p.949, n.1.

Saunier, Charles: see Ba30.4.

Bb474 Savarus, Pierre de, in *Trois jours en Belgique*, Paris: Dentu, 1876, pp.33-48.

Bb475 Schaffer, Aaron, 'The Louvre and EF', *South Atlantic Quarterly*, XXII (Oct. 1923), 370-5.

Bb476 Schapiro, Meyer, 'F as a critic', *Partisan Review* (Jan. 1949), 25-51.

Bb477 Schérer, Edmond, *'Dominique'*, *Le Temps* (17.6.1862).

Bb478 ——, ['EF'], *Le Temps* (5.9.1876); repr. in *Etudes sur la littérature contemporaine*, Paris: Lévy, 1878, vol. V, pp.251-86.

Bb479 ——, 'EF', *Le Courrier Littéraire* (10.7.1877). Text of a lecture given in Versailles (11.4.1877).

Bb480 Schlumberger, Jean, 'Notes et chroniques (1910-1911)', in *Œuvres*, Paris: Gallimard, 1958, vol. I, p.199.

Bb481 Schneider, René, Ref. in *L'Art français: du réalisme à notre temps*, Paris: Laurens, 1930, pp.60-1.

Bb482 Scurr, Gérald, 'La Rochelle: F and the East', *The Connoisseur*, CLXXIV, 702, p.277.

Bb483 Séailles, Gabriel, in *L'Origine et les destinées de l'art*, Paris: Félix Alcan, 1925, pp.107-8.

Bb484 Seillière, Ernest, 'Morale romantique et morale bourgeoise', in *Pour le centenaire du Romantisme*, Paris: Champion, 1927, pp.180-2.

Bb485 Sells, A. Lytton, 'A Disciple of *Obermann*: EF', *Modern Language Review*, XXXVI, 1 (Jan. 1941), 68-85.

Sévegrand, Maria: see Ab16.

Bb486 Seznec, Jean, 'Odilon Redon and literature', in *French 19th-Century Painting and Literature*, ed. Ulrich Finke, Manchester: Manchester University Press, 1972, p.286. See also *ibid.*, p.298.

Bb487 Silvestre, Armand, in *Portraits et souvenirs (1886-1891)*, Paris: Charpentier, 1891, pp.111-30.

Silvestre de Sacy, Samuel: see Ab26.

Bb488   Simon, Pierre-Henri, 'Lettres d'Aunis et de Saintonge', in *La Charente-Maritime*, Paris: Edns J. Delmas et Cie, 1968, Coll. 'Richesses de France', 2nd edn, pp.142-5, 147, 150-1.

Bb489   Sloane, Joseph C., in *French Painting between the Past and the Present: Artists, critics and traditions from 1848 to 1870*, Princeton: Princeton Univ. Press, 1951, pp.206 (n.26), 208-9.

Bb490   Smith, Garnet, 'EF', *The Magazine of Art* (Oct. 1895), 454-60.

Bb491   Sonolet, Louis, 'F critique d'art', in Ba30, pp.62-72.

Bb492   —, 'EF', *La Quinzaine* (16.10.1905), 538-55.

Bb493   —, 'Le Centenaire de notre F', in Ba18, pp.36-43.

Bb494   —, 'Le Centenaire d'EF', *Journal des Débats* (25.10.1920).

Bb495   Souday, Paul, 'Chronique littéraire: EF, *Lettres de jeunesse*', *L'Opinion* (18.9.1909), 376-8.

Bb496   —, 'Les Livres: EF', *Le Temps* (29.10.1920).

Bb497   —, 'Le Cinquantenaire de F', *Le Temps* (6.9.1926).

Bb498   Souquet, Paul, 'EF', *La Nouvelle Revue*, IV (15.2.1881), 866-85.

Bb499   Sourioux-Picard, Suzanne, 'Sous le signe d'Aunis', *Vie Contemporaine* (Feb. 1933).

Bb500   —, '*Dominique*, ou le chef-d'œuvre qui dure', *La Parenthèse* (May 1934).

Bb501   —, 'Chez leurs descendants', *Vendémiaire* (24.1.1936).

Bb502   Spronck, Maurice, 'Le Centenaire d'EF', *L'Eclair* (24.10.1920).

            Stewart, Caroline: see Ab10.

Bb503   Storzer, Gerald H., in 'The Fictional Confession of Adolescent Love: A Study of Seven Romantic Novels' [Chateaubriand, *Atala*, *René*; Balzac, *Le Lys dans la vallée*; Constant, *Adophe*; F, *Dominique*; Nodier, *La Fée aux miettes*; Nerval, *Aurélia*], Ph.D. thesis, Univ. of Wisconsin, 1967, pp.14, 93, 99-121, 177, 185-9, 192, 193, 198, 199, 203, 205.

Bb504   Strowski, Fortunat, 'Voyage en Egypte', *Le Quotidien* (31.3.1936).

Bb505   Suire, Louis, in *Le Paysage charentais dans l'œuvre d'EF et de Pierre Loti*, La Rochelle: A la Rose des Vents, 1946, *passim*.

Bb506   —, Refs in *Le Charme de La Rochelle*, La Rochelle: A la Rose des Vents, 1965, pp.38-9, 60, 82-4.

Bb507 —, 'EF, peintre et écrivain', lecture given at the Musée d'Aquitaine de Bordeaux (11.12.1965; 12.12.1965).

Bb508 Sully-Prudhomme, Armand, in *Journal intime: lettres – pensées*, Paris: Lemerre, 1922, pp.162-3.

Bb509 Sutton, Howard, 'Two Confessions: *Adophe* and *Dominique*', *The American Society Legion of Honor Magazine*, XL, 2 (1969), 85-98.

Bb510 Tadié, Jean-Yves, Refs in *Introduction à la vie littéraire du XIXe siècle*, Paris & Montreal: Bordas, 1970, Coll. Etudes Supérieures, Section littéraire dirigée par Jean Céard, pp.17, 35, 37.

Bb511 Taine, Hippolyte, 'Lettre à Edouard de Suckau [15 juin 1862]', in *H. Taine, sa vie et sa correspondance*, Paris: Hachette, 1904, vol. II, p.255.

Bb512 Talva, Jean, 'La Culture du souvenir: à propos des lettres de jeunesse d'EF', *NRF* (1.9.1909), 121-9.

Bb513 Talvart, Hector [see also Ba1], 'F écrivain', *Courrier de La Rochelle* (14.2.1909).

Bb514 —, 'Discours prononcé sur la tombe d'EF' [in the cemetery of Saint-Maurice (5.11.1926)], *Annales de l'Académie de La Rochelle* (1927), 56-60.

Bb515 —, 'Pierre Loti, EF et la terre natale', *Cahiers de Climatologie* (15.10.1934).

Bb516 —, 'L'Ame tragique de Pierre Loti', in *Images de Pierre Loti* [with François Duhoureau & Gaston Mauberger], La Rochelle, Edns d'Art 'Ramuntcho', 1935, pp.13-20.

Bb517 —, Refs in *L'Ame du Pays d'Ouest: Poitou-Charentes*, La Rochelle: A la Rose des Vents, 1943, pp.52-4 & *passim*.

Bb518 Tarbel, Jean, 'EF', *La Nouvelle Revue* (1.3.1905), 24-8.

Bb519 Taslitzky, Boris, 'Plaidoyer pour EF', *La Nouvelle Critique* (Dec. 1957), 151-6.

Bb520 Tharaud, Jérôme & Jean, 'L'Afrique vue par F', in Ba18, pp.28-9.

Bb521 Thibaudet, Albert, 'F', *Revue de Paris*, XXVII (Oct. 1920), 760-89; (Nov. 1920), 149-84; repr. in Ba34.

Bb522 Thierry, Edouard, 'Revue littéraire', *Le Moniteur Universel* (7.7.1857).

Thoré, Théophile: pseudonym of W. Bürger (q.v.).

Bb523   Timbal, Charles, in *Notes et causeries sur l'art et sur les artistes*, Paris: Plon, 1881, pp.326-8.

Bb524   Trapadoux, Charles, '*Un Eté dans le Sahara*', *Revue Contemporaine* (30.5.1857), 809-13.

Bb525   Trarieux, Gabriel, 'EF paysagiste', in Ba30, pp.28-33.

Bb526   Traz, Robert de, '*Dominique* ou l'honneur bourgeois', *Esprits Nouveaux* (Aug. - Sept. 1922); repr. in *Essais et analyses*, Paris: Crès, 1926, pp.145-66.

Bb527   Trudgian, Helen,   Refs in *L'Esthétique de J. -K. Huysmans*, Paris: Conard, 1934, pp.107-8.

Bb528   Vandérem, Fernand, 'Le Centenaire de F et *Dominique*', *Les Lettres et la Vie* (15.3.1921); repr. in *Le Miroir des lettres*, Paris: Flammarion, [1922], Ser. IV, 1921, pp.14-23.

Bb529   —, 'Le Cinquantenaire de F', in *Le Miroir des lettres*, Paris: Flammarion, 1929, Ser. VIII, 1925-1926, pp.266-7.

Van de Waal, H.: see Ab48.

Bb530   Vanet, André, 'EF', in *Variations...*, La Rochelle: Imprimerie Saintard, 1948, pp.9-26. Text of a lecture given in La Rochelle (7.9.1947).

Bb531   Van Gogh, Vincent,   Refs in *Lettres à son frère Théo*, Paris: Grasset, 1937, pp.18, 108, 109.

Bb532   Vathel, Jean, 'Les Peintres rochelais au Salon de 1864', *La Revue de l'Aunis* (1.7.1864), 543-5.

Bb533   Vaudoyer, Jean-Louis, 'F et le roman d'amour', *Le Gaulois* (5.11.1920).

Bb534   —, in *En France*, Paris: Plon, 1933, pp.39-43.

Bb535   Vaux de Foletier, François de, 'Les Ancêtres de F', *Mercure de France*, CCXCIV, 989 (Aug. - Sept. 1939),333-47.

Bb536   Venoize, Maurice, 'EF orientaliste', *Revue France-Islam*, II, 21 (Sept. 1924).*

Bb537   Venturi, Lionello,   Refs in *Histoire de la critique d'art* [tr. from the Italian by Juliette Bertrand], Paris: Flammarion, 1969, pp.31, 241, 249, 252-3, 256.

Bb538   Vianey, Joseph, 'L'Œuvre littéraire d'EF', in *Discours prononcé à la rentrée solennelle des Facultés de l'Université de*

Montpellier, Montpellier: Delord, Boehm & Martial, 1903. Text of an address given in Montpellier (3.11.1903).

Bb539 Vier, Jacques, 'Le *Dominique* de F, roman de désintoxication romantique', *L'Ecole* (5.5.1951), 362, 383-4; (19.5.1951), 385-6, 407; also in Ba36, pp.39-53.

Bb540 ——, 'Pour l'étude du *Dominique* de F', *L'Ecole* (19.2.1955), 325-9; (5.3.1955), 360-2, 383-4; (16.4.1955), 453-5; also in Ba36, pp.1-38.

Bb541 Vignaud, Jean, 'La Véritable Histoire de *Dominique*', in *Demeures inspirées et sites romanesques*, textes et documents réunis par Paul-Emile Cadilhac & Robert Coiplet, Paris: Les Edns de 'l'Illustration', 1958, vol. III, pp.183-8.

Bb542 Villes, René, 'F et son roman: *Dominique*', *Intermédiaire des Chercheurs*, XXVII (10.3.1893), 247.

Bb543 Vincens, Charles, 'EF', *Revue Politique et Littéraire*, XI, 14 (30.9.1876), 315-9.

Bb544 Viollet-le-Duc, E., 'EF', *Journal des Débats* (24.10.1876).

Bb545 Virolle, R., 'Explication de texte. F: Dominique au phare', *L'Ecole* (16.4.1960), 535-6.

Bb546 Vosmaer, C., 'Un Mot à propos de Rembrandt', *L'Art*, V (1876), 166-7.

Bb547 Waille, Victor, 'Le Monument de F', *Revue Africaine*, (1903), 312-34.

Bb548 Wais, Kurt, 'Die Existenz als dichterisches Thema im Fs *Dominique*', *Zeitschrift für französische Sprache und Literatur*, LXVI (1956), 202-22; repr. in *Französische Marksteine von Racine bis Saint-John Perse*, Berlin: Gruyter, 1958, pp.223-44.

Bb549 Warnod, Jeanine, 'F: le peintre et l'écrivain (Exposition de La Rochelle)', *Le Figaro* (4.7.1970).

Bb550 West, C.B., 'Notes on *Dominique*', *French Studies*, IX, 2 (April 1955), 116-28.

Bb551 ——, CR of Ba9, *Modern Language Review*, LXI (1966), 712-3.

Bb552 Wiarda, R., Refs in *Taine et la Hollande*, Paris: Droz, 1938, pp.242-51.*

Bb553 Wilmotte, Maurice, 'EF et les réalistes', *La Revue Latine* (25.1.1903), 46-58; repr. in *Etudes critiques sur la tradition littéraire en France*, Paris: Champion, 1909, pp.283-303.

Bb554 Wolff, Albert, in *La Capitale de l'art*, Paris: Victor-Havard, 1886, pp.129-42.

Bb555 Wright, Barbara [see also Ab3, 23, 25, 38; Ac13], 'F, poète et paysagiste de l'Ouest (d'après des documents inédits)', *Revue du Bas-Poitou et des Provinces de l'Ouest*, LXXIV, 3 (1963), 175-94.

Bb556 ——, 'F's Concept of Creative Vision in the Manuscript of *Dominique*', *French Studies*, XVIII, 3 (1964), 213-26.

Bb557 ——, 'The Suggestive Art of F', paper read to Research Seminar, Univ. of Exeter (11.12.1964).

Bb558 ——, CR of Ba9, *French Studies*, XIX, 3 (1965), 306-8.

Bb559 ——, '*Valdieu*: A Forgotten Precursor of F's *Dominique*', *Modern Language Review*, LX, 4 (1965), 520-8.

Bb560 ——, 'L'Art d'EF', lecture given to the Alliance française de Dublin (13.10.1967).

Bb561 ——, 'La Dédicace de *Dominique*', *Studi Francesi*, XXXV (1968), 302-5.

Bb562 ——, CR of Ab28, *French Studies*, XXIII, 1 (1969), 84-5.

Bb563 ——, 'F et Le Verrier: un incident révélé par des lettres inédites', *Studi Francesi*, XL (1970), 75-6.

Bb564 ——, 'Introduction à l'aspect littéraire de l'œuvre d'EF', in Ba7, pp.xv-xx; repr. in Ba31, pp.19-24.

Bb565 ——, 'Gustave Moreau and EF: a reassessment of their relationship in the light of new documentation', public lecture given at Trinity College, Dublin (29.10.1971); account given in *Hibernia*, XXXVI, 20 (5.11.1971), 17; see also *Irish Times* (29.10.1971).

Bb566 ——, 'From Reality to Fiction: The Origins of *Dominique* in the Correspondence of F', lecture given to the Royal Irish Academy (28.2.1972).

Bb567 ——, 'Gustave Moreau and EF: a reassessment of their relationship in the light of new documentation', *The Connoisseur*, CLXXX, 725 (1972), 191-7. Abridged version of Bb565.

Bb568 Wyzewa, Théodore de, Ref. in *Les Maîtres italiens d'autrefois*, Paris: Perrin, 1907, p.273.

Bb569 ——, 'Le Carnet de voyage d'EF', *Le Temps* (28.7.1911).

Bb570 Zola, Emile, Refs in *Salons*, ed. F. W. J. Hemmings & Robert J. Niess, Geneva & Paris: Droz & Minard, 1959, pp.39, 55, 56, 77, 188-9, 193.

Bb571 Anon., 'Le Cinquantenaire de F', *La Gazette d'Aunis* (7.11.1926; 17.11.1926).

Bb572 —, 'Le Cinquantenaire d'EF', *L'Echo Rochelais* (10.11.1926).

Bb573 —, 'Un Curieux Document sur deux ouvrages de F', *Bulletin du Bibliophile* (March 1927).

Bb574 —, 'Ferdinand Humbert élève de F', *La Gazette d'Aunis* (17.4.1935).*

Bb575 —, in *Le Roman réaliste et naturaliste: F, Flaubert, les Goncourt, A. Daudet, Zola*, Paris: Didier, 1939, Les Grands Ecrivains de France illustrés, pp.3-11.

Bb576 —, 'Romance and Character' [CR of Ab17], *Times Literary Supplement* (20.11.1948), 649.

Bb577 —, 'A Polished Mirror', *Times Literary Supplement* (17.2.1950), 104.

Bb578 —, CR of Ab25, *Bulletin Critique du Livre Français*, XXII, 3 (March 1967), 206-7.

Bb579 —, 'Juin - Juillet - Août, La Rochelle se prépare à célébrer le 150e anniversaire de la naissance d'EF (1820-1876)', *Le Sud-Ouest* (28.5.1970).

Bb580 —, 'L'Hommage de l'Académie des Belles-Lettres à EF', *Le Sud-Ouest* (12.6.1970).

Bb581 —, 'F, écrivain et peintre', *Amateur de l'Art* (25.6.1970).

Bb582 —, CR of Ac13, *Bulletin Critique du Livre Français* (May 1972), No. 1999.

Bb583 —, CR of Ac13, *GBA* (May - June 1972).